The Relationship Between the Baptism with the Spirit and the Isaianic New Exodus

The Relationship Between the Baptism with the Spirit and the Isaianic New Exodus

WALTER RAY NUTT

Foreword by Rick Wadholm Jr.

WIPF & STOCK · Eugene, Oregon

THE RELATIONSHIP BETWEEN THE BAPTISM WITH THE SPIRIT
AND THE ISAIANIC NEW EXODUS

Copyright © 2025 Walter Ray Nutt. All rights reserved. Except for brief quotations in critical publications or reviews, no part of this book may be reproduced in any manner without prior written permission from the publisher. Write: Permissions, Wipf and Stock Publishers, 199 W. 8th Ave., Suite 3, Eugene, OR 97401.

Wipf & Stock
An Imprint of Wipf and Stock Publishers
199 W. 8th Ave., Suite 3
Eugene, OR 97401

www.wipfandstock.com

PAPERBACK ISBN: 979-8-3852-4183-5
HARDCOVER ISBN: 979-8-3852-4184-2
EBOOK ISBN: 979-8-3852-4185-9

VERSION NUMBER 042825

Unless otherwise noted, Scripture quotations are from the New American Standard Bible®, 1971 edition, Copyright © 1960, 1971, 1977, 1995, 2020 by The Lockman Foundation. All rights reserved.

To my wife
Flora Burgos Nutt

Contents

Foreword by Rick Wadholm Jr. | ix
Preface | xiii
Acknowledgments | xx
List of Abbreviations | xxi

Chapter 1
Introduction | 1

Chapter 2
Review of Literature | 10

Chapter 3
Exegesis of Luke | 81

Chapter 4
Results and Conclusion | 116

Bibliography | 127

Foreword

PENTECOSTALS HISTORICALLY HOLD TO a functional canon-within-the-canon of Luke-Acts. This is not to say that Pentecostals have often intentionally or knowingly committed to this (though some have), but that the hermeneutical and theological practice has defaulted to this. The foundational commitment to the doctrine of the baptism with/in the Spirit predisposes Pentecostals to such. Luke-Acts is the functional matrix of texts by which the classical Pentecostal movement has heard other texts of Scripture including Paul and the rest of the NT (much as Anabaptists traditionally hear the Sermon on the Mount in a similar fashion), and this is nowhere more keenly felt than in the doctrine of the baptism with/in the Spirit.

In particular, the Pentecostal doctrine of the baptism includes two emphases that draw upon the narratives of Acts even as also being dependent upon other philosophical (epistemological) foundations: the evidentiary function of tongues and the separability of the baptism from salvation. This first of these is typically expressed by the language of "initial physical evidence" to indicate that tongues is chronologically tied in close proximity to the baptism (to such an extent that the popular testimonial discourse seems to collapse the baptism and tongues into one another's horizons) and demonstrates outwardly the received testimony for the community to affirm this one has indeed received the baptism. Numerous other evidences are expected as long-term outcomes (such as power for witnessing to Jesus, etc.) and as inward transformations of the baptized (such as greater love for the Scriptures and the Lord), but it is tongues that is functional for the initial affirmation that this one has received the baptism.

As to the second emphasis, the issue of separability between the baptism and salvation, Pentecostals have confessionally rejected collapsing the baptism into salvation. The two function in ways that make the crisis experiences associated with each of them to be separable events (even when in very close chronological sequence in Scripture or contemporary experiences). This seems to function to dissuade Pentecostals from casting aspersions at those not giving evidence of the baptism as if they were not actually saved (though within the broader scope of Pentecostalisms, the Oneness Pentecostals argue it as part of the Acts 2:38 *ordo salutis*: salvation, water baptism in Jesus' name, and baptism in the Spirit). Separability further functions to highlight the uniqueness of the baptism from the experience of salvation as a distinct experience and thus as a call to seek more from the Lord in the life of the Spirit. It is a call for a further experience of the Spirit.

Luke-Acts is *the* biblical collection heard first and foremost for the Pentecostal distinctive of "initial physical evidence (or sign)" concerning the baptism in/with the Spirit (this being the precise language of a majority of Pentecostal statements of faith, though not all). After all, it is Acts that offers the Lukan paradigmatic repetitions of explicit testimonial texts indicating speaking in tongues as indicative of Spirit reception (2:4; 10:44–47; 19:6) with a further two implicit accounts (8:15–18; 9:16 heard with 1 Cor 14:18) functioning as some manner of evidence to the literary audience of reception of the Spirit.

Long before the work of Roger Stronstad's *The Charismatic Theology of St. Luke* was published Pentecostals had already assumed the theological intent of Luke in his writings. Stronstad simply provided a stronger hermeneutical basis to inform the Pentecostal presuppositions as intending tongues to function for the earliest Jesus followers as evidence of their baptism. The further intentional theological reading of Luke-Acts opened the way for further studies.

Enter the work you are reading by Walter Nutt. He has taken up the task of rehearing Luke-Acts as a Pentecostal and within the Pentecostal context in relation to the Isaianic new exodus (INE). This INE has also become widely recognized in Lukan scholarship, and in this way, Nutt is not offering something novel. However, where he does open up a fresh conversation is in his bringing INE into conversation with the Pentecostal baptism with the Spirit in Luke-Acts.

For Nutt, the INE is programmatic for hearing the very texts which have long been heard by Pentecostals in support of their doctrine of the baptism. In this way, Nutt proposes that the emphasis on "separability" has created an unnecessary boundary to a broader experience within Pentecostal congregations of the baptism. All too often the baptism has become relegated to an addition that helps but does not belong to the essential intent of the Lord. The emphasis on separability has further proven to separate the life of Jesus as playing out in this New Exodus as if it were only moments instead of a continuous flow of God's life-giving Spirit to set all things to rights. It has treated it as if these were not the same outflow of the purpose of Jesus to set things right. In these ways, the theological separability has led to a wider chronological separability between the experience of salvation and the baptism even when it is testified to by tongues.

In this volume, Nutt offers a bold prophetic call to experience the baptism as God's purpose revealed in Luke-Acts rather than to argue over issues of separability. Not everyone will be convinced by his reading, but all should wrestle with this prophetic call. He offers ways in which Isaiah's message is heard in continuity and fulfillment through Luke-Acts. The baptism is argued to be Luke's intent throughout his work. To miss the thrust of the Lukan texts is to miss the intent that the Spirit be poured out on all flesh by the Lord Jesus as the programmatic intent of Jesus' life, death, resurrection, and exaltation. Jesus came to baptize with the Spirit. To miss this is to miss the intent of God to deliver, heal, restore, resurrect, and make all things new by means of the Spirit poured out to the ends of the earth in witness to the Lord's reign.

For Nutt, the baptism is not optional or a tack-on. The baptism belongs to the very heart of the God of Israel to carry out his purposes on earth as in heaven. Further, the baptism is taken up as the outflow along the story of Israel as God's plan all along taken up in the Lord Jesus. In this way the story of the Spirit-baptized bearing witness from Jerusalem to the ends of the earth is the story of the INE. It is the story of Israel. It is the story of Jesus. It is the story of the church. The first and last of these taken up together in the Spirit-baptized, Spirit-baptizer. There is no end that does not entail the Spirit poured out and overflowing.

Hear the call: Receive the Spirit! This is for you and your children and all who are far off!

Rev. Rick Wadholm Jr., PhD
Associate Professor of Old Testament
Assemblies of God Theological Seminary
Springfield, MO, USA

Preface

DR. BENNY AKER STATES, "This proposes to be a good and necessary study. There are some important issues addressed—to show what the baptism of Spirit is and how it fits with the Isaianic new exodus is one of them. Pentecostals have not connected Spirit baptism with Isaiah (even Joel in Acts 2 fits into Isaiah's new exodus). This has not been done. This will be an eye opener for Pentecostals and can generate more studies and papers."[1]

This dissertation was presented to Global University in Springfield, Missouri, in partial fulfillment for a doctor of ministry in biblical studies and theology. It seeks the meaning of the "baptism with the Holy Spirit" in relation to the new covenant. It seeks to find Luke's theme and argument; to place the events of Acts chapter 2 within the argument; and to determine its meaning. Luke's use of promise and fulfillment throughout guides the study to his use of the Old Testament as central to solving the problem.

The literature review provides the working hypothesis that the most probable design for Luke-Acts is the Isaianic new exodus. From the beginning and through the narrative, Luke presupposes the arrival of the new eschatological era described in Isaiah. The narrative emphasized the temple and Jerusalem as significant to its main theme.

The Isaianic new exodus is the new covenant promise to the remnant of Israel and includes the restoration and reunification of Israel and the inclusion of the gentiles within the people of God.

---

1. Interview with Dr. Ben Aker (March 2022).

This is what Acts 1:8 promises. It is the outline—hermeneutical grid—for Luke-Acts in correlation with the INE. In this light, the baptism with the Spirit is explained as a multidimensional work that comprised the totality of Jesus' ministry involving many manifestations of the Holy Spirit such as conviction, repentance, cleansing and new life, sanctification, filling[2] for missions/prophetic ministry, and growing in the grace of God. Pentecostal baptism (filling with the Spirit) is the capstone of the new exodus. To say that conversion and filling are not the same but connected in the process defends the biblical point. What this does is unify experientially God's process of evangelizing the whole world. Missions from transformed Israel to the gentiles, e.g., ends of the earth, is what Luke is saying about Isaiah's message.

The author is a fourth-generation Pentecostal believer. Pentecostal baptism is considered as a real experience and is not an issue addressed in this study. The emphasis is on Luke's following of Isaiah with emphasis on the whole work of Jesus. There has not been an adequate study on how the Spirit connects salvation and Pentecostal baptism. The Spirit is manifested more fully in the believer who is "baptized in the Spirit," but it is the same Spirit at work in the believer. "Missions" is embedded in the new life, and the experience of salvation has brought a new relationship with God. It only becomes more prominent when the believer is "Spirit-filled."

Object of the Study

THIS STUDY SEEKS TO find the meaning of the baptism with the Spirit as it relates to Jesus's life and the Pentecostal filling in the upper room in Jerusalem (Acts 2). It explains the meaning of the Pentecost event by using Luke's Isaianic new exodus design as the research variable. It will search for meaning in the structure of the text of Luke-Acts following the INE identity story to determine the

---

2. Pentecostal baptism.

significance of the Pentecost event of Acts chapter 2 and provide a renewed understanding of Pentecost for today.

Research Design

The research design focuses on the praxis, the stories, and the symbols that characterize Jesus's ministry and what the Old Testament teaches through the INE. We will follow the historical-critical/grammatical method described by Craig Blomberg. Accordingly, this study proceeds to analyze the historical setting in which the book of Luke-Acts occurs including earlier written sources and whatever distinctive emphases the author of the document may have added to the tradition inherited.

The objective is to ascertain the author-encoded historical meaning.[3] It considers that the main source that the author and his recipients shared was the Old Testament and more specifically the identity story of Israel—i.e., INE. This dissertation analyzes Luke-Acts, including earlier written sources to bring light on the distinctive emphases of Luke. Finally, the historical-critical/grammatical method consists of word studies, grammatical forms, sentence parts, sentences, and multi-sentence structures as they relate to each other.

We will follow Leland Ryken's approach to the genre of a biblical narrative for principles that govern the interpretation of the narrative unity of the Bible. The Bible is taken as a whole; the Bible tells a story that has a beginning, a middle, and an end.[4] Corresponding to the narrative nature of the Bible is its chronological nature. The major units can be arranged in an unfolding sequence.

Beale's biblical theological method[5] will guide the use of the Old Testament in the New. He outlines five presuppositions that Jesus, the apostles, and the early church followed in interpreting the Old Testament. First, they assumed "corporate solidarity of

---

3. Klein, Blomberg, and Hubbard, *Introduction to Biblical Interpretation*, 185.

4. Ryken, *Words of Delight*, 31.

5. Beale, *New Testament Use of the Old Testament*, loc. 2062.

representation." Second, they understood that Christ served as the representative head for the entire community of faith throughout history, including all true believers in Israel. Third, they believed that "history is unified by a wise and sovereign plan so that the earlier parts are designed to correspond and point to the latter parts." Fourth, they recognized that the "age of eschatological fulfillment" had been inaugurated (but not yet fully realized in Christ). Finally, they concluded that the earlier stages of biblical history should be interpreted within the larger, canonical context of its later stages. In other words, they believed that Christ and his glory were the end-time center and goal of redemptive history and the key to interpreting the Old Testament. Beale considers that the "noncontextual methods are illegitimate."[6]

Ryken states that "there is a discourse level to the stories of the Bible."[7] How storytellers induce readers to move from the setting, action, and characters of a story to the meaning is called rhetorical criticism (analysis of the persuasive strategies of the storyteller). Ryken notes that the setting, the plot, and the characters should all correspond.[8] The question should simply be, What is the relationship between the setting and the characters and events of the story? We will attempt to place Pentecost within Luke's argument in the rhetorical text.

Stargel's social identity approach[9] is also incorporated, which states that the exodus narratives with a literary setting in every major socio-cultural transition in Israel's larger story portray Israel's rehearsal of and participation in exodus as central and essential to her ongoing collective identity. The exodus story preserves the identity of Israel and projects future events. The exodus theme is repeated throughout the Old Testament and reaffirmed by Luke using Isaiah's eschatologized version of the exodus narrative, which includes Abrahamic, Mosaic, and Davidic themes.

---

6. Beale, *New Testament Use of the Old Testament*, loc. 283.
7. Ryken, *Words of Delight*, 53.
8. Ryken, *Words of Delight*, 55.
9. Stargel, *Construction of Exodus Identity*, loc. 3762.

This study will be historical, literary, and theological in nature. The exegetical study is classified partially as a conceptual historical, literary-critical, theological research study. Conceptual historical research is concerned with the origin, development, and influence of ideas and concepts.[10] The study of Luke-Acts is diachronically seeking foremost to understand the meaning for Luke and its original readers in light of previously written Scripture.

The historical analysis will study Luke's presentation of Jesus's story and the outpoured Spirit. It is important that as Son of God, what he understood as his role and purpose are assumed to be true. The inquiry follows the process from action to mindset, from mindset to action. This forms the process in which history does its work. Wright states that variations within a worldview, in the form of particular mindsets, can and do occur at all levels (symbol, story, praxis, questions, beliefs, aims, and intentions), but they become especially public and visible when they emerge in words or actions.[11]

The basic assumption of the study is that the author of Luke-Acts was not simply a collator of sources but also a skilled writer. He was a theologian with a purpose in what he wrote. The work employs a careful reading of the context and co-text to determine the meaning of the "baptism with the Holy Spirit" and its relation to the covenant throughout. Also, a theological discussion surrounding the issue of separability and distinction between the work of the Spirit in salvation and other activities of the Spirit will be necessary. Other related theological subjects will also be addressed (i.e., covenant, salvation) in the study.

Rationale

I selected this study problem because of its potential for the edification of the church. It seemed like much of the previous work treating Pentecostal theology was apologetically oriented. A fresh,

---

10. Leedy and Ormrod, *Practical Research*, 177.
11. Wright, *Jesus and the Victory of God*, loc. 3106.

objective, exegetical study of the Scripture from the Pentecostal viewpoint is needed. Attempting to defend the traditional Pentecostal point of view, scholars have narrowed the scope of the Spirit's work. This can be enhanced by addressing the role of Jerusalem in Luke-Acts. Jerusalem was the center of operations of the Davidic kingdom. It is there that YHWH restores Israel and judges between the remnant and the idolatrous leaders in Israel. Attention to the role of Isaiah and the new exodus in Luke-Acts will clarify the significance of the Pentecostal event.

Luke's underlying framework and its relation to the new exodus theme are ascertained using accepted tools of exegetical analysis that are qualitative. The data is gathered through careful readings and exegesis of the new exodus narratives in Luke-Acts.

Sources for the Study

The primary source is the Nestle Aland twenty-eighth edition and the UBS third edition of the Greek text of Luke-Acts and its Old Testament quotations in the Hebrew or Septuagint text. Any variants that may affect meaning will be addressed, and discrepancies between the Hebrew text and the LXX will be resolved. For the study of the text, Old Testament quotations will be identified in Luke and examined in (both) context(s) to identify Luke's argument and meaning. The major positions will be surveyed in the existing literature to form a review and a theoretical and conceptual framework. Select exemplar texts from the Greek text of Luke-Acts will be analyzed as related to the subproblems to identify a pattern that will clarify the meaning of the baptism with the Spirit concerning the covenant as described in the INE.

Proposed Chapters of the Report

The research report chapters will be as follows: chapter 1: introductory material including the statement of the problem and the research questions; chapter 2: a literature review including pertinent literature on the subproblems of the research project; chapter 3: the exegesis and results section covering the text of Luke-Acts through the lens of the INE theme; chapter 4: summary, conclusions, and recommendations for further study.

Acknowledgments

SPECIAL THANKS TO MY mentor—Dr. Benny Aker. Without his timely guidance, this dissertation would lack focus and depth. His perceptive criticism and expertise on points requiring further study and argumentation have immeasurably improved the quality of this work. Prof. Aker has provided an exemplary model of creative and rigorous scholarship that has given me direction for the years to come.

I also acknowledge the influence of my godly parents who provided a home conducive to biblical scholarship. My mother's sensitivity to the Spirit and passion for ministry have kept me close to the Lord through challenging times. My mother was buried in Bolivia. My father is still in Bolivia teaching and preaching faithfully—since 1969—still going forward.

I recognize Global University with each of the graduate faculty that have added to my formation. Every step I encountered godly men and women who invested in my life.

List of Abbreviations

BDAG	Bauer, Walter, William F. Arndt, and F. Wilbur Gingrich, *The Greek Lexicon of the New Testament and Other Christian Literature*
DBL	*Dictionary of Biblical Languages: Greek New Testament*, James Swanson
DI	Deutero-Isaiah—Isaiah 40–55
INE	Isaianic new exodus
LES	Lexham English Septuagint
LXX	Greek Septuagint version of the Old Testament
NA[28]	Nestle Aland Greek New Testament 28th edition
NIDNTTE	*New International Dictionary of New Testament Theology and Exegesis*
NT	New Testament
OT	Old Testament
PI	Proto-Isaiah—what Isaiah 1–39 is known as
TDNT	*Theological Dictionary of the New Testament*
TI	Trito-Isaiah—Isaiah 56–66
UBS	United Bible Societies Greek New Testament, 3rd edition
WOL	Way of the Lord

Chapter 1

Introduction

THEOLOGY EITHER DRIVES AND encourages experience or not. Larry Martin describes an early Pentecostal experience, "After a study of the book of Acts, the students entered a time of prayer and waiting on God. On January 1, 1901, Agnes Nevada Ozman, a thirty-year-old student, received the Baptism in the Holy Spirit with the evidence of speaking in a language she did not know (known as glossolalia)."[1] William and Robert Menzies qualify Ozman's experience as having occurred with "conscious theological understanding" of the event.[2]

The study of the "baptism with the Holy Spirit"[3] needs a renewed conscious theological understanding based on current scholarship and a fresh reading of Scripture. Historically Pentecostals assumed an apologetic stance defending the baptism with the Spirit. It was necessary to provide biblical support for the Pentecostal baptism as an experience subsequent to the conversion

---

1. Martin, *In the Beginning*, 19. Martin gathers his evidence from Agnes N. O. LaBerge, *What God Hath Wrought in My Life* (Chicago: Herald, n.d.).

2. Menzies and Menzies, *Spirit and Power*, 16.

3. Lukan metaphors for the Spirit are many ("clothed"—ἐνδύσησθε in Luke 24:49; "fell upon"—ἐπέπεσεν in Acts 10:44; "filled"—πλησθῆς in Acts 9:17; "came upon"—ἦλθε τὸ πνεῦμα τὸ ἅγιον ἐπ' αὐτοῖς in Acts 19:6).

initiation experience. The "filling" with the Spirit[4] comes at the crown or apex of the new exodus. It is united in the process, and believers should seek filling immediately upon coming to Christ. Luke (from Jesus no less) sets forth, in particular, Isaiah's prophetic outline of God's eschatological work. Conversion and filling with the Spirit are not the same but connected in the process. Overemphasis on separability tends to drive a wedge between Passover and Pentecost and drives away the Pentecostal experience (initial and subsequent fillings with the Spirit). Missions from the transformed Israel to the gentiles, e.g., ends of the earth, is what Luke is saying about Isaiah's message all unified in the process of the Isaianic new exodus.

Problem Statement

What is the relationship between Holy Spirit baptism and the covenant? Pentecostal theology has overemphasized the "baptism with the Holy Spirit" as theologically disconnected from regeneration[5] to show subsequence. This stems from a limited view of the baptism with the Holy Spirit (using the term to relate only to Pentecostal baptism) and results from an apologetic stance.[6] According to John Wyckoff, Pentecostals have made a strong argument for subsequence to prove separability and distinctiveness and thus validate the experience.[7] The experience does not need validation; it needs to be received. What is necessary is to properly understand Luke's use of Isaiah as his hermeneutical grid to show the fulfillment of prophecy in what Jesus came to do and continues to do today.

Historically, there was a need to argue for an experience that was disconnected from salvation. Anthony D. Palma concludes that the emphasis of responsible Pentecostals has always been on

---

4. Luke prefers the word "filling" throughout Acts.

5. See also Wyckoff, "Baptism in the Holy Spirit," loc. 597; Palma, *Holy Spirit*, loc. 1797.

6. Riggs, *Spirit Himself*, loc. 211; Fee, "Baptism in the Holy Spirit," 87–99.

7. Wyckoff, "Baptism in the Holy Spirit," loc. 9420.

theological separability, not temporal subsequence.[8] Subsequence was emphasized to prove theological separability. If both regeneration and Spirit baptism are included in the new covenant, why then, is the baptism theologically disconnected? Why does Pentecostal baptism have to be theologically distinct to be considered subsequent to the conversion initiation experience?

The twentieth-century Pentecostal revival had a beginning date in 1901. It follows that the first theologians of the movement would seek to validate the experience theologically in the light of their original beliefs. This produced language that was apologetic. William and Robert Menzies[9] describe both the charismatic renewal of the 1950s and the rapprochement between Pentecostals and Evangelicals that required a defense of the Pentecostal experience.[10]

This apologetic stance has caused overemphasis on Luke's portrayal of the Spirit of prophecy[11] and has resulted in the neglect of Luke's main argument. By emphasizing that Luke had a different theological stance than Paul, Pentecostals have argued for a baptism for initiation and incorporation (Paul) and a baptism for charismatic speech and gifting (Luke).

Subproblem One: Theme, Purpose, and Argument of Luke-Acts

Identifying the overall theme and argument of Luke-Acts in the light of recent scholarship is important to place the ministry of Jesus and the day of Pentecost within Luke's historical narrative

---

8. Palma, *Holy Spirit*, loc. 1797.

9. Menzies and Menzies, *Spirit and Power*, 130.

10. Fee ("Baptism in the Holy Spirit," 87–99) argues that "since Pentecostals have regularly argued for the biblical nature of both their experience of baptism and its timing (as separate and subsequent), making the timing of equal significance to the experience itself, those who have opposed the Pentecostal position have also generally believed to have dealt a crippling blow to Pentecostalism when they have argued exegetically against its timing."

11. Menzies, "Luke's Understanding of Baptism," 108–26.

and theology. There is a consensus among scholars[12] today that the structure of Luke-Acts has theological significance.[13] Luke said that he wrote an orderly account of the things that had been fulfilled. Luke's orderly account was not just a rehearsal of historical facts; rather, it was a theological explanation of how it all fulfilled what they already knew and expected from the Old Testament account. Luke's explanation of recent events provides a theological (therefore also didactic and normative) explanation to the historical events recorded in the book of Acts.

Subproblem Two: Luke's Use of the Old Testament

Recent scholarship has tried the Isaianic new exodus (INE) as a probable paradigm for Luke's writings. Benny Aker states that "scholars are realizing that both Luke-Acts and John depended especially upon Isaiah 40–55 for their stories of Jesus and the Spirit."[14] Pentecostal scholars have not explored the meaning of the baptism with the Spirit as related to Luke's use of the INE as structure for his work. This study surveys existing literature to find an all-inclusive theme and argument of Luke-Acts. The details are defined in view of the overarching theme.

Subproblem Three: The Meaning of Baptism with the Holy Spirit

The phrase "He himself will baptize you with the Holy Spirit and fire" (Luke 3:16)[15] is the significant passage for understanding the meaning of baptism with the Spirit in the ministry of Jesus. The context for Luke 3:16 is the book of Isaiah which unifies the

---

12. See chapter 2, "Review of Literature."

13. Keener, *Acts: Exegetical Commentary* 1:722; Pao, *Acts and the Isaianic New Exodus*, 1–16; Bock, *Theology of Luke and Acts*, loc. 682; Tannehill, *Narrative Unity*, loc. 93.

14. Aker, "Charismata," 53–69.

15. Translation mine.

identity story of Israel and conditions the narrative as well as the inclusion of other Old Testament texts and concepts in Luke-Acts.

There is discrepancy between theologians as to the meaning of the preposition ἐν in the phrase "He shall baptize you with the Holy Spirit and fire." Pentecostals have used "baptism in the Spirit." This represents a theological stance and a limited definition of Spirit baptism. Is the baptism with the Spirit and fire limited to the day of Pentecost and beyond (traditional view), or is it a description of all of Jesus's ministry? If it is a description of all of Jesus's ministry, then Luke's preference for "filling" in Acts 2:4— ἐπλήσθησαν πάντες πνεύματος ἁγίου[16] ("they were all filled with the Holy Spirit")—is validated.[17]

Subproblem Four: Meaning of Jerusalem and the Temple

Throughout Luke-Acts, Luke emphasizes Jerusalem. Pentecostals have not explored the meaning of Jerusalem in relation to Jesus's ministry and the Spirit. Something was going to happen in Jerusalem, and its significance was central to the meaning of the covenant. It is in Jerusalem that one finds for sure that Luke is spelling out the new exodus. He gets it from Isaiah.

Purpose of the Study

The purpose of the study is to identify the main theme and subthemes of Luke-Acts and define the phrase "He himself will baptize you with the Holy Spirit and fire"[18] in the light of his purpose and argument. It is argued that the initial apologetic stance of Pentecostals needed to defend Pentecostal baptism has contributed to Pentecostals ignoring Luke's argument and does not properly describe the ministry of the Spirit that Luke portrays. It has made the baptism ("filling" for Luke) of the Spirit more than

---

16. Aland et al., *Greek New Testament*, Acts 2:4.
17. Translation mine.
18. Luke 3:16, translation mine.

just disconnected theologically and semantically; it has also made it experientially rare. The filling (baptism) of/with the Spirit has become an optional, exclusive experience rather than for "you and your children and for all who are far off."[19]

Research Questions

1. What is the main theme of Luke-Acts? Is it related to the covenant?
2. If the argument of Luke-Acts is based on the Isaianic new exodus (hereafter INE), how does it affect terminology and Pentecostal hermeneutics related to Spirit baptism?
3. What is the meaning of "baptize with the Holy Spirit and fire" in the context of John's and Jesus's ministries and Luke's use of Isaiah to describe it?
4. Why does Luke emphasize Jerusalem?

Importance of the Study

There is a need for Pentecostal theology to be updated with a fresh approach that defines Luke's work based on his explanation of history and its continuity with the Old Testament. It is necessary to develop an approach that is the result of a fresh reading of Scripture based on current scholarship. Robert Menzies represents traditional Pentecostal theology when he states,

> Pentecostals, then, recognize that the New Testament speaks of two baptisms in the Spirit—one that is soteriological and initiates the believer into the body of Christ (1 Cor 12:13) and one that is missiological and empowers the believer for service (Acts 1:8). However, Pentecostals feel that it is particularly appropriate to adopt Luke's language and speak of the Pentecostal gift as a "baptism

---

19. Acts 2:39, translation mine.

in the Holy Spirit" . . . . Pentecostals fear that if Paul's language is employed and the gift of the Spirit received at conversion is designated "the baptism in the Holy Spirit," then a proper understanding of the Pentecostal gift will be lost.[20]

William and Robert Menzies state that the future of the movement is uncertain. They attribute it to the fact that the "theological legacy of Pentecostalism is ambiguous. Pentecostals have been known for their spiritual vitality, not their theological prowess or intellectual rigor." They further state that, "paradoxically, just as the Pentecostal movement faces this significant theological challenge, so also it finds itself with unparalleled opportunities for fresh theological reflection."[21] It is to this challenge that this study rises.

What does Scripture record? Luke draws a parallel from the Old Testament and portrays the promise and fulfillment of the promised plan. A Pentecostal believer has experiential evidence; however, there is a responsibility to be true to the Scriptures and responsibly pass on the results of diligent study to the next generation of Pentecostal believers to bring about a renewed wave of Spirit-fillings.

Limitations and Delimitations of the Study

1. This study will concentrate on the Greek text of Luke-Acts and Isaiah[22] and secondary sources related to solving the problem.
2. The English text used throughout the study is the New American Standard Bible version, 1971 edition.
3. Luke-Acts will be analyzed as it relates to Isaiah. Scripture passages from other Old Testament and New Testament books will be used when relevant.

---

20. Menzies, "Luke's Understanding of Baptism," 126.
21. Menzies and Menzies, *Spirit and Power*, 9.
22. Septuagint (LXX).

Assumptions

1. Luke is taken as the author of the two-volume work "Luke-Acts."²³
2. Experiential presuppositions are important;²⁴ however, they are not the starting point.
3. Luke follows the Septuagint closely. Conzelmann suggests that this is not by chance—Luke makes a conscious effort to write in a devotional and biblical style. He writes in a literary Greek style as is evidenced by distinct features such as the use of the optative, rare in the New Testament (5:24; 8:31; 10:17; 17:18; 17:27; 20:16; 25:16; 26:29). He also uses rhetorical devices unique to literary Greek as well as Hellenistic Greek forms (i.e., his fondness for double expressions is characteristic of the LXX, especially the Maccabees).²⁵ It is a given that Luke's main source for the Old Testament was the Septuagint.²⁶
4. Isaiah is taken as a unit. It is agreed that Isaiah has at least three main segments: Isaiah 1–39 (PI), 40–55 (DI), and 56–66 (TI) to conform to sources cited or to refer to them. Even though there has been discussion of multiple authors, in recent times, Isaiah's thematic unity has become more apparent. Brevard Childs states, "The message of Second Isaiah cannot be properly understood apart from First Isaiah. The testimony of Second Isaiah is concerning the events of history which usher in the new age of redemption that has been previously announced."²⁷ He argues for the unity of Isaiah. His approach is taken here. Mark Strauss notes that the New

---

23. Stronstad, *Charismatic Theology of St. Luke*, 4; Marshall, *Acts*, 60; Bock, *Theology of Luke and Acts*, loc. 789.

24. Stronstad, *Spirit, Scripture, and Theology*, 61.

25. Allen, *Lukan Authorship of Hebrews*, 43; Pao, *Acts and the Isaianic New Exodus*, 5.

26. Bovon, *Luke the Theologian*, 94; Park, *Pentecost and Sinai*, 177.

27. Childs, *Introduction to the Old Testament*, 328.

Testament authors quoted from the book as one.[28] Seijin Park states that Luke would not have understood the modern historical-critical division of Isaiah into First, Second, and Third Isaiah.[29]

5. Normativeness as characteristic of the genre of Luke's historiography is accepted.[30] Substantial work has been done on the normative character of Acts by Roger Stronstad.[31] "Pentecostals emphasize the normative theological intent of Luke's historical record of the gift of the Spirit for contemporary Christian experience."[32] Stronstad states that the historical narratives of the Old Testament served as a model for Luke's historiography.

6. The Pentecostal phenomenon of glossolalia are considered the initial evidence of Pentecostal baptism; however, this subject is beyond the scope of this study and will not be considered.

---

28. Strauss, *Davidic Messiah in Luke Acts*, 236.

29. Park, *Pentecost and Sinai*, 179.

30. John Stott, *Baptism and Fullness*, loc. 184, argues against using the narrative of Acts as basis for establishing normativeness of the Pentecostal experience (cf. Fee, "Baptism in the Holy Spirit"). He states that the narrative must be interpreted according to didactic portions of Scripture and the teaching of Jesus. The INE as theological structure of Luke-Acts provides the interpretation needed for the narrative.

31. Stronstad, *Charismatic Theology of St. Luke*, 7.

32. Stronstad, *Charismatic Theology of St. Luke*, 5.

Chapter 2

Review of Literature

THE SUBPROBLEMS RELEVANT TO this literature review are the theme, purpose, and argument of Luke-Acts, Luke's use of the Old Testament, the meaning of the baptism with the Holy Spirit and fire in Lukan pneumatology, and the significance of Jerusalem for Luke. The objective is to research the subject on the relationship between the covenant and the baptism with the Holy Spirit.

Subproblem One: Theme, Purpose, and Argument of Luke-Acts

Theme and Purpose

The prologue of Luke is explicit as to the purpose of the writing. In Luke 1:1–4, Luke proposes to write an orderly account that would bring certainty to Theophilus regarding the things he had been taught. This implies that Luke was presenting the facts with a certain scheme in mind. Varied themes and purposes have been proposed historically for Luke-Acts. Most authors propose a main theme and sub-themes. This study seeks a theme and structure that is all-inclusive of the various themes and sub-themes proposed.

Fulfillment of the Promise. Walter Kaiser Jr. takes the position that, since the church was undergoing persecution, those like Theophilus may have wondered if the promise-plan of God was still in force.[1] All that Jesus had done and would do was according to divine necessity (δει)[2] and to God's everlasting plan. Even though not all the occurrences of δει in Luke-Acts are used to show divine necessity (i.e., Luke 13:14; Acts 15:5; 27:26), many are (Luke 2:49; 4:43; 9:22; 13:16; 17:25; 21:9; 24:7, 26, 44; Acts 17:3). The divine necessity theme shows that the events in Christ's life or in the life of the church were not haphazard. There was a divine urgency and guidance.[3] The fulfillment of the promise-plan of God is a major theme of Luke-Acts.[4]

John Squires uses God's providential guidance as the underlying theme showing how related themes of Spirit, divine agents, miracles, fulfillment, and necessity are linked with explicit statements of God's plan and fulfillment of the promise.[5] In Acts 2:23, Peter claims that Jesus's crucifixion occurred as part of God's "predetermined plan and foreknowledge"[6] (τῇ ὡρισμένῃ βουλῇ καί προγνώσει τοῦ θεοῦ). The plan of God has a central role in Luke-Acts because it is related to the crucial events in the story which Luke narrates, namely the passion of Jesus and the mission to the gentiles. Luke uses Spirit, divine agents, miracles, fulfilment, necessity, and God's providential guidance to provide a comprehensive interpretation of the plan of God in the history of the early church.

Keener considers Luke's approach to Scripture as being key to understanding his theological perspective. He argues that the gentile mission was a legitimate extension of Israel's faith. "Luke presents the biblical heritage positively, emphasizing continuity

---

1. Kaiser, *Promise-Plan of God*, 317.
2. Used forty times in Luke-Acts.
3. Kaiser, *Promise-Plan of God*, 320.
4. Carson and Moo, *Introduction to the New Testament*, 158; Liefeld, *Interpreting the Book of Acts*, 118; Bock, *Theology of Luke and Acts*, loc. 691; Keener, *Acts: Exegetical Commentary*, 1:438.
5. Squires, "Plan of God in the Acts of the Apostles," 22.
6. Translation mine.

with this heritage wherever possible... Luke finds in Israel's Scripture both promises and patterns fulfilled in his day."[7] For Luke, the ministry of Jesus, the Jesus movement, and the gentile mission are the fulfillment and continuation of the biblical story.

Salvation for the Nations. There is consensus that salvation is the main purpose of Luke-Acts. Bock shows the theme of Luke-Acts as a detailed discussion of God's plan in which salvation is for all because Jesus is Lord of all.[8] For Derek Morphew the purpose of Luke-Acts is the arrival of the messianic king who by the power of the Spirit brings healing and salvation to all nations.[9] Marshall shows continuity in the story of the early church emphasizing that Luke's central concern is salvation. He shows how the theological emphases in Luke arrange themselves naturally around the broad theme of the purpose of God to bring salvation to Jews and gentiles alike through Jesus the Prophet and Messiah.[10]

For Marshall, the missionary element is Luke's foremost concern.[11] Strauss follows this line emphasizing that the mission to the gentiles was God-ordained and central to God's plan for human history.[12] Flattery argues that Luke set out to write a reliable account of how God's plan was fulfilled according to promise. He sees the primary purpose as having to do with the salvation of the nations.[13] Luke wrote history with the purpose of evangelizing and expressing sound theology.[14]

Legitimacy. Marshall suggests that all other purposes are subordinate to the main theme of the presentation of the historical

7. Keener, *Acts: Exegetical Commentary*, 1:491.
8. Bock, *Acts*, 63.
9. Morphew, *Mission of the Kingdom*, 31.
10. Marshall, *Acts*, 23.
11. Marshall, *Acts*, 37.
12. Strauss, "Purpose of Acts," 447.
13. Flattery, *Holy Spirit in the New Testament*, 15.
14. Strauss, "Purpose of Acts," 344.

basis (legitimacy) of the Christian faith.[15] Bock traces Luke's claim for legitimacy through Jewish heritage as the main purpose.[16] The claim for heritage was important for new movements. By showing that there were promise and fulfillment of the events, the Christian movement could be viewed as a continuation of Judaism and not something new and suspicious.[17] Bock states that "Luke-Acts showed that the coming of Jesus launched the long-promised new movement of God."[18]

Richard Pervo characterizes it as a "legitimating narrative."[19] He states that from Aristotle's time forward, a major reason for composing the history of a subject has been the bestowal of legitimacy upon it. Jesus was dead; although, many witnesses saw him alive and ascending into heaven. The Holy Spirit had been poured out just as the prophets had said would happen when the new covenant came. And most troubling, the church/restored remnant was full of gentiles. This needed explaining and the whole movement legitimized.

Witherington includes the legitimacy question. "How can Christianity be the true Israel of God when it is rejected by Jews and so few Jewish have been converted to it?"[20] Perhaps Theophilus was asking how it could be legitimate if the Roman state also opposed and persecuted the church (e.g., Acts 18). Luke had to show that "the Way" was no innovation but was predestined by God.

Multiple Purposes. Luke writes to make certain the things that were known. This can mean different things. Carson and Moo list several purposes that Luke might have considered in writing:

15. Marshall, *Acts*, 22.
16. Bock, "Scripture and the Realization," 49.
17. Morphew, *Mission of the Kingdom*, 31.
18. Bock, *Theology of Luke and Acts*, 29. See also Reist, "Theological Significance of the Exodus," 231.
19. Pervo, *Acts*, 21.
20. Witherington, *Acts*, 74.

(a) to conciliate Jews and gentiles; (b) evangelism/apologetics; (c) theological polemics; and (d) to edify Christians.[21] Theophilus and all like him needed to be assured that no amount of persecution could be interpreted as a sign of God's judgment or that the promise-plan of God had failed.

Pao provides multiple facets to the purpose of Luke-Acts: (a) to strengthen the faith of readers; (b) to deal with the delay in the *parousia*; (c) a defense of Christianity; (d) a proclamation of the gospel of salvation; and (e) the universality of God's salvation and the impact of such salvation on the identity of God's people.[22]

Argument of Luke-Acts

Summary Statements as Structure Indicators. Keener includes a section on "Summary Statements" when discussing the structure of Luke's work. He asserts that Luke had a structure because "appropriate arrangement of material was a primary concern for those who were rhetorically sensitive."[23] According to Keener's summary, these summary statements can be narrowed to six that are closely related to the gospel's expansion (6:7; 9:31; 12:24; 16:5; 19:20; 28:31). These would divide Acts into six panels:

1. 1:1—6:7 The church in Jerusalem
2. 6:8—9:31 Judea and Samaria (e.g., 1:8)
3. 9:32—12:24 To gentiles (a nongeographic category)
4. 12:25—16:5 Asia and the shift to emphasizing the gentile mission
5. 16:6—19:20 Urban centers in Europe (returning also to Ephesus)
6. 19:21—28:31 To Rome

Geographical Progression as Structure. Concerning the structure of Luke, Kaiser sees a geographical progression theme.[24] First,

---

21. Carson and Moo, *Introduction to the New Testament*, 301–5.
22. Pao, *Commentary on Acts*, loc. 216.
23. Keener, *Acts: Exegetical Commentary*, 1:574.
24. Kaiser, *Promise-Plan of God*, 321.

the infancy narratives and the ministry of John the Baptist (Luke 1:1—4:13), then, Luke emphasizes Jesus's Galilean ministry (Luke 4:14—9:50). From that point on, Jesus was headed to Jerusalem (Luke 9:51; 13:33; 17:11; 18:31). After that, the narrative proceeds to the passion, resurrection, and ascension narratives (Luke 19:45—24:53). In like manner, there is a geographical progression in Acts. It is laid out in Acts 1:8. The movement was from Jerusalem to Judea, to Samaria, and the ends of the earth.

Neudorfer demonstrates that Luke used a structure that had geographical criteria in mind.[25] Luke emphasizes in Luke-Acts how the gospel prompts human beings to act and become mobile. In Stephen's speech, Luke uses words to show this concept with OT examples ("come out," ἐξέρχομαι, v. 7; "sent out," ἐξαποστέλλω, vv. 12, 14, 34, 35; "lead out," ἐξάγω, vv. 36, 39; "coming," ἔλευσις, v. 52).[26] Luke chose these words deliberately to teach readiness to change both geographically and ideologically.

Speeches. Hans Bayer sees the structure of Acts as relating to the speeches of Peter.[27] The ones that are paradigmatic for the book of Acts are the sermons at Pentecost and the temple. Bayer claims that on a literary level, the speeches interact with the aim of the narrative in a reciprocal and explanatory fashion. "Peter arises as a prophetic repentance preacher along the lines of Old Testament calls to return to the God of the Fathers."[28] The speeches of Acts contribute to the literary structure and development of thought

---

25. Neudorfer, "Speech of Stephen," 279.
26. Translation mine.
27. Bayer, "Preaching of Peter in Acts," 258.
28. Bayer, "Preaching of Peter in Acts," 257.

(e.g., Peter: Acts 2:14–36, 38–40; 3:12–26; 10:34–43; Paul: Acts 13:16–41).

The Holy Spirit. The Spirit is an underlying subject in Luke-Acts. Robert Menzies lists several parallels between Jesus's experience with the Spirit and that of the disciples. These include:

1) Both accounts are placed at the beginning;
2) both associate the reception of the Spirit with prayer;
3) both record audible and visible manifestations;
4) both offer explanations of the event in the form of a sermon that alludes to the fulfillment of Old Testament prophecy.[29]

Luke presents Jesus's reception of the Spirit as a model for the disciples in Acts and a future generation of believers.

James Shelton suggests that Luke has superimposed the structure of early church pneumatology upon the synoptic material. In the light of the outpouring of the Holy Spirit upon all flesh—Jews and gentiles alike—Luke reinterpreted the synoptic material in hindsight. According to Shelton, Luke sees John and other participants in the infancy narrative as speaking by means of the Holy Spirit in identical terms used in Acts and in the church era. Shelton argues for this based on Luke's use of the phrase "filled with the Holy Spirit" from the beginning and throughout.[30]

Kaiser writes on the importance of the Holy Spirit in the promised plan of God.[31] At his baptism, the Spirit descended on Jesus. This marked the beginning of his earthly ministry. In the same manner, the baptism with the Holy Spirit marked the beginning of the church. The two parts of Luke's story are parallel. The phrase "filled with the Spirit" marks intervals in Luke-Acts. Even before Jesus's birth, the Holy Spirit was emphasized. Further on, Stephen spoke of a sin that had to do with "resisting the Spirit" just as their fathers had done (Acts 7:51).

29. Menzies, "Luke's Understanding of Baptism," 116.
30. Shelton, *Mighty in Word and Deed*, 25.
31. Kaiser, *Promise-Plan of God*, 323.

Isaianic New Exodus. Scholars have explored the INE as a possible argument of Luke-Acts. Ruthven states,

> Isaiah 59:19–21 provides not only a prediction of the Pentecost events but imposes a sequential and thematic coherence on Acts 2. Thus, Isaiah 59:19–21 serves as the programmatic statement for the book of Acts building upon its mirrored programmatic passage (Isa 61:1–2) of Luke's first volume. In Luke, Jesus is the bearer of the Spirit, in Acts, he is the bestower of the Spirit.[32]

Ruthven sees the main theme of Luke to be the INE.

Pao offers the extended quotation of Isa 40:3–5 at the beginning of Jesus's public ministry as the "hermeneutical key" through which the rest of the Lukan narrative is to be understood.[33] In Acts 1:8, Luke supplied a programmatic statement for the development of the narrative. He discussed the motifs in the prologue in Isa 40:1–11 that play a critical role in the narrative of Acts. The prologue of Isa 40–55 (hereafter DI) introduces the main themes of the coming new exodus. Pao points to five passages in which the programmatic use of these themes frames Luke's narrative: Luke 4:16–30; 24:44–49; Acts 1:8; 13:46–52; and 28:25–28.[34]

According to table 1 on the structure of Luke-Acts, the text has many literary forms as well as parallels to the Old Testament.

Table 1. Structure of Luke-Acts

Theme	Academic Support	Description	Supporting Scripture
Summary Statements	Keener	Divides Luke into six panels.	Luke 6:7; 9:31; 12:24; 16:5; 19:20

---

32. Ruthven, "This Is My Covenant with Them (Part II)," 219.
33. Pao, *Acts and the Isaianic New Exodus*, 37.
34. Pao, *Acts and the Isaianic New Exodus*, 109.

Geographic Progression	Kaiser	Based on the travel narratives (1) infancy narratives (2) Galilean ministry (3) Jesus was headed to Jerusalem (4) Passion, resurrection, and ascension narratives.	Luke 1:1—4:13; Luke 4:14—9:50; Luke 9:51; 13:33; 17:11; 18:31; Luke 19:45—24:53
Speeches	Bayer	On a literary level, the speeches interact with the aim of the narrative in a reciprocal and explanatory fashion.	Acts 2:14-36; Acts 3:19-21; Acts 7:2-53; Acts 13:16-41
Lukan Pneumatology	Shelton	Luke has superimposed the structure of early church pneumatology upon the synoptic material.	Text of Luke-Acts
Holy Spirit	Morphew Menzies Kaiser	Parallels sought between Jesus's experience of the Spirit and that of Pentecost.	Luke 3:21, 22; Acts 2:4
Isaianic New Exodus	Ruthven Pao Anderson Watts Wright	Luke follows the Isaianic new exodus in the structure of Luke-Acts.	Isa 40:3-5; Isa 59:19-21; Luke 4:16-30; 24:44-49; Acts 1:8; 13:46-57; and 29:25-28

The INE as a proposed structure and explanation of the history of Jesus's ministry and that of the early church has merit and will be tested in this study. The INE includes the themes in the other proposed plans.

Subproblem Two: Luke's Use of the Old Testament

It has been suggested that Christian Pentecost is related to the covenant on Mount Sinai (Park, VanderKam). Others maintain that the kingdom of David motif informs Luke's writing (Hahn, Harris, O'Toole, Strauss, Wright). Still others emphasize Luke's use of the covenant either to realign readers in their relationship and identity with Israel or simply as a fulfillment of prophecy (Kent, Kovacs, Sanders, Kaiser). The INE motif is also prevalent among Lukan scholars (Ruthven, Pao, Kwon, Harris, Manek, Turner, Wilms, Wright). Still others address the issue of whether the Holy Spirit in Acts is poured out for soteriological or missiological emphasis (Loder, Menzies, Marshall, Stronstad, and Turner). These different emphases will be considered as a part of Luke's use of the Old Testament in the literature review.

Isaianic New Exodus as the Argument of Luke-Acts

The Consolation of Israel. The opening section of Isa 40:1-2 contains a call for comfort (consolation). It is the same word used by Simeon upon the arrival of Jesus in the temple (Luke 2:25). Benny Aker states, "Isaiah 40:1-2 contains the significant text that sets forth the entire enterprise of new exodus deliverance in terms of 'comfort' or 'consolation' (LXX *paraklēsis*, paraclete)."[35] Pao states that in the context of Isa 40-55, "comfort" entails an act of God on behalf of his people.[36]

Laying Claim to an Ancient Tradition. Pao argues that Isa 40 and the INE serve as a hermeneutical lens without which the entire Lukan program cannot be properly understood.[37] Isaiah 40:1-11 functions as the prologue for Isa 40-55 and, as such, sets the stage for the various themes presented. The themes of Isa 40:1-11

---

35. Aker, "Paraclete," loc. 7492.
36. Pao, *Acts and the Isaianic New Exodus*, 46.
37. Pao, *Acts and the Isaianic New Exodus*, 5.

correspond to the ones controlling the narrative of Acts. These themes include the consolation of Israel, the universal revelation of the glory/salvation of the Lord, the power of the word of God, and the restoration of the people of God. Even though Pao structures his discussion on chapters 40–55, the INE theme occurs throughout Isaiah.

Pao states that Luke constructed the narrative of the development of early Christianity within the framework of the INE to lay claim to the ancient Israelite tradition.[38] Acts 1:8 corresponds to the stages in Isaiah's program. In Isaiah's three-part program there is (a) the arrival of the salvation of God in Jerusalem (Isa 40:1–2), (b) the restoration and reunification of Israel (Isa 40:9–11), and (c) the mission to the gentiles (Isa 40:3–5).[39] All of these are present in the Acts 1:8 paradigmatic statement referring to the restoration of the kingdom.

The Hermeneutical Framework of Luke-Acts. The Isaianic program is the hermeneutical framework in which isolated events are interpreted. In Luke 4:16–30, Luke introduces the framework in which his writings should be understood.

> The Spirit of the Lord is upon Me,
> Because He anointed Me to preach the gospel to the poor.
> He has sent Me to proclaim release to the captives,
> And recovery of sight to the blind,
> To set free those who are downtrodden,
> To proclaim the favorable year of the Lord.

All five clauses in this Isaianic quotation refer to the arrival of the salvation of God. This allows Luke to emphasize the new era as a legitimate continuation of the history of the people of God.

Pao states that the same paradigm provided by Isaiah is used in the Lukan writings where the identity of the early Christian

---

38. Pao, *Acts and the Isaianic New Exodus*, 93. See also Park, *Pentecost and Sinai*, 179.

39. Pao, *Commentary on Acts*, loc. 238.

movement is being questioned.⁴⁰ Luke 24:44-49 alludes to Isa 49:6 and justifies a move toward the gentiles and the redefinition of the people of God. Acts 1:8 is programmatic for the rest of the book. Acts 13:46-47 is also programmatic. It is an important passage for redefining the people of God beyond Israel. Acts 28:25-28 quotes Isa 6:9-10 and emphasizes the rejection of the Jews and the turning to the gentiles. Luke emphasizes the restoration of Israel as well as the legitimate inclusion of the gentiles within the plan of salvation based on the INE.

Keener suggests that making the INE the primary scriptural grid for Luke-Acts may limit Luke; however, "Isaiah proves to be the most critical grid for the narrative's movement to Gentiles, making Pao's contribution one of the most helpful recent studies on Acts."[41] He states that Isaiah provides most of the programmatic statements but is not the only narrative subtext.

Luke quotes Amos 9:11: "After this, I will return and will rebuild the dwelling of David, which has fallen; from its ruins, I will rebuild it, and I will set it up, so that other peoples may seek the Lord—even all the Gentiles over whom my name has been called" (Acts 15:16). In other words, it is time for the gentiles to come in, because Israel's exile is at last over, and she has been restored—i.e., the INE.

After the Pentecost narrative of Acts 2, Peter cites the INE ("this promise is for you and your children and for those who are afar off"). Ruthven considers this verse as the cornerstone of the new covenant for the book of Acts.[42] Isaiah 59:20-21 is a promise of the new covenant. Ruthven concludes that Isa 61:1-2 is programmatic for Luke and Isa 59:19-21 is programmatic for Acts. His position includes the following:

1. Powerful rushing sound of wind/Spirit. "For He will come like a rushing stream, which the wind of the Lord drives" (Isa 59:19). "And when the day of Pentecost had come, they were

---

40. Pao, *Acts and the Isaianic New Exodus*, 34.
41. Keener, *Acts: Exegetical Commentary*, 1:482.
42. Ruthven, "This Is My Covenant with Them (Part I)," 32.

all together in one place. And suddenly, there came from heaven a noise like a violent, rushing wind, and it filled the whole house where they were sitting" (Acts 2:1).

2. Words/inspired speech. "My words which I have put in your mouth, shall not depart from your mouth, nor from the mouth of your offspring," says the Lord, "from now and forever" (Isa 59:21). Luke reiterates the emphasis of Isaiah on the relationship of the promised Spirit and speech often in Acts. "They were all filled with the Holy Spirit and began to speak in other tongues, as the Spirit gave them utterance" (Acts 2:4). Being "filled" resulted in words, a sequence that follows Isa 59:21, "My Spirit which is upon you, and my words which I have put in your mouth . . . The word 'filling' makes it clear that the speech-giving Spirit was inside the recipients—hence the words were in their mouths as Isaiah described."[43]

3. Fear of the Lord. Ruthven sees that there is a cause-and-effect connection between the rushing mighty wind and the "attentively fearful reaction of the international audience."[44] The description of this fearful reaction shows Luke's dependence upon Isa 59. He states,

> The universal fear of the Lord of Isaiah 59:19 (from the west, and from the rising of the sun) is alluded to in Acts chapter two. The word "wonder" in its verb form identifies the response of the multitude to the theophanic events of Pentecost. . . . But in its nominal use the word seems to extend this response to the celestial events of Joel ("wonders . . . and signs") the "signs and wonders" of the exalted Jesus (Acts 2:22) and the "wonders and signs" of the apostles (Acts 2:43).[45]

---

43. Ruthven, "This Is My Covenant with Them (Part I)," 40.
44. Ruthven, "This Is My Covenant with Them (Part I)," 42.
45. Ruthven, "This Is My Covenant with Them (Part I)," 45.

The Promise of the Spirit and the Covenant. With regard to the covenant and the INE theme, Ruthven states,

> The first action of the redeemer was to come in theophanic wonder (Isa. 59:19; Acts 2:2, 23–39), secondly, to come in this way specifically to Zion/Jerusalem (Isa 59:20; Luke 24:45–49; Acts 1:4), and thereby to cause repentance to Jacob/Israel (Isa 59:20b; Acts 2:35–38), all this is to produce the climactic purpose of the Pentecost narrative; the ongoing bestowal of the covenantal Spirit.[46]

In Acts 2:17, Luke uses the phrase "the last days" to describe the arrival of the new exodus and the radical shift (i.e., transformation) of history to a new era.

Ruthven shows how Luke substitutes the word διαθήκη (LXX) with ἐπαγγελία—of the Spirit (Luke 24:49; Acts 1:4; 2:33; 3:19; Isa 59:21).[47] He states,

> In this Luke seems to follow biblical usage generally, where ἐπαγγελία refers to "covenant": Rom 4.13–14, 20; 9.4,8; 2 Cor 6.16–7.1; Gal 3.14–17, 29; 4.23–28; Eph 1.13; 2.12; 3.6; Heb. 4.1; 6.12, 13, 15, 17; 7.6; 11.9, 13, 17; 8.6; 9.15; 10.36; 11.39; 2 Pet 3.9. . . . In Peter's direct quotation of the Isaiah prophecy, the substitution for "covenant" is clear: "This 'promise' (ἐπαγγελία) (covenant) is to you and to your children and to all who are afar off" (2:39). If we substitute "covenant" for Luke's "promise" regarding the outpouring of the Spirit, then the theme of Isaiah 59 fulfillment is even clearer (Luke 24:49; Acts 1:4; 2:33).[48]

Peter's invitation to repent, be baptized, and receive the Holy Spirit follows Isa 59:21: "My Spirit which is upon you, and My words which I have put in your mouth, shall not depart from your mouth, nor from of the mouth of your offspring, nor from the mouth of your offspring's offspring, says the LORD, from now and forever."

---

46. Ruthven, "This Is My Covenant with Them (Part II)," 230.
47. Ruthven, "This Is My Covenant with Them (Part II)," 230.
48. Ruthven, "This Is My Covenant with Them (Part II)," 230.

Israel's Collective Identity Story. Linda M. Stargel states that the exodus narratives are part of Israel's ongoing collective identity.[49] Every major socio-cultural transition in Israel's history includes a rehearsal and participation in the exodus story. The primary exodus story has two aspects that support its ongoing presence in Israel. First, the story includes instruction to commemorate (Exod 12:14–20), remember, and tell (10:2; 12:25–27). Second, the story concludes with a poetic paradigmatic song that invites ongoing participation in Exod 15:1–21. This is indicative of the chief purpose of the narrative to emphasize the importance of persistent, ongoing participation of Israel in the exodus.

Even those who had never been in Egypt were meant to see themselves as having been liberated from bondage. Throughout the Old Testament, the exodus is repeated with each later generation being portrayed as those who experienced the exodus. In Deut 6:25, when future generations ask the meaning of everything, they should respond, "We were Pharaoh's slaves in Egypt, but the LORD brought us out of Egypt with a mighty hand" (Deut 26:5–9; Josh 24:2–7; Ps 136:10–15, 23–24). The personal pronouns portray the inclusion of later generations in "the people whom God brought out of Egypt."[50]

Richard J. Clifford proposes that there is a single narrative or identity story throughout the history of Israel that can be called the "national story" of Israel. He says that this story existed in two ideal types, one "historic" and the other "cosmogonic."[51] The difference between the two depends on the prevalence of divine and human actors and earthly and heavenly perspectives.

According to Clifford, the cosmogonic version consists of YHWH battling hostile forces such as the sea or desert and leading the people out of peril. The historic version gives prominence to humans such as Moses and Joshua. Existing literature mixes both types due to historical details being found in cosmogonic versions and vice versa. The writing prophets prefer the historic type. Isaiah

---

49. Stargel, *Construction of Exodus Identity*, loc. 6152.
50. Stargel, *Construction of Exodus Identity*, loc. 156.
51. Clifford, *Fair Spoken and Persuading*, 13–21.

40–55 retells the national story; however, he differs from other writing prophets because of his movement between the historic and cosmogonic types. The fusion of the exodus-conquest and the cosmogonic version of Israel's story produces the "new event" of a new exodus.

The exodus from Egypt formed a part of Israel's identity story. YHWH had delivered his people from bondage "with a mighty hand and an outstretched arm" (e.g., Isa 40:10; 51:9; 52:10). His glory would be revealed to all flesh (40:5) for all nations would behold the miracles of the new exodus. During the first exodus, the Lord went before them and guarded the rear (Exod 13:21–22; 14:19–20). Isaiah 52:12 states, "For the Lord will go before you, and the God of Israel will be your rear guard."

Bernard Anderson lists the motifs of the sacred history that Second Isaiah reinterpreted eschatologically: the promises to the fathers, the deliverance from Egypt, the journey through the wilderness, and re-entry into the promised land.[52] Like a warrior, like a man of war (Isa 42:13; e.g., Exod 15:3) YHWH will fight for his people. He caused "chariot and horse . . . to lie down together and not rise again" (Isa 43:16–17; e.g., Exod 14:28; 15:10–21). In a like manner, YHWH will overcome all of Israel's oppressors (Isa 49:24–26; 51:22–23; 52:3–6) and accompany the new exodus with a victory song—like Moses's and Miriam's song after the deliverance at the sea (Isa 42:10–13; e.g., Exod 15:21; e.g., Rev 4:9–14).

Just as in the original exodus, YHWH will lead his people (Isa 42:16; 48:20; 49:9–10; 52:12). And again, YHWH will defeat the horse and the chariot at the sea in his role as a mighty warrior (Isa 40:10; 42:13; 43:16–17; 51:9–10; 52:10; e.g., Exod 14:25, 28; 15:3). Just as YHWH led Israel through the parted sea, YHWH will lead his people through the waters (Isa 43:1–2; 51:10). Finally, YHWH will provide food and water in the wilderness (Isa 41:17–20; 43:19–21; 48:21; 49:9–10).

Scot McKnight shows that Paul considered that the story of Jesus "fulfills, completes, and resolves Israel's story." "Salvation— the robust salvation of God—is the intended result of the gospel

---

52. Anderson, "Exodus Typology in Second Isaiah," 177–95.

story about Jesus Christ that completes the Story of Israel in the Old Testament." When Paul says "according to the Scriptures" he means the whole of the Old Testament witness to the atonement. McKnight argues that Jesus believed the "kingdom of God was breaking into history."[53] Second, Jesus declares a new society in the land. Third, Jesus declares a new citizenship. He shows how the Lukan Beatitudes make a clear distinction between those who are "in" and those who are "out." Jesus believed and declared that he was at the center of the kingdom of God. McKnight states, "The startling implications of Luke 4:16–30, the opening preaching scene for Jesus, is that he had the ego to think that Isaiah's words from chapter 61 were finding their way to him as their fulfillment."[54]

The Promised Plan of God is the INE. Mark Strauss notes that the concept of an eschatological new exodus is not a New Testament interpretation inspired by the Exodus themes; rather, the theme was already developed in the Prophets, especially in Isaiah.[55] While Israel may look to its origins in the first exodus, Isaiah transformed the identity story into a future hope. Isaiah prepared the way for the New Testament author's understanding of the relation between the cross, Pentecost, and the promised plan of God.

Bryan Estelle offers several possible functions of the INE motif.[56] First, an emphasis on YHWH as the divine sovereign emerges. Recounting YHWH's past actions and events of Israel assures the people that God will do new and wonderful things on their behalf. This story motivated those in Babylon, the later New Testament reader, and the modern reader.

A second function is the recalling of the universal blessings promised to Abraham. The promises of the covenant of grace revealed to Abraham were coming true (i.e., that through him all the nations of the earth would be blessed). This theme emerges

---

53. McKnight, *Jesus Gospel*, loc. 1450.
54. McKnight, *Jesus Gospel*, loc. 1516.
55. Strauss, *Davidic Messiah in Luke Acts*, 285.
56. Estelle, "Exodus Motif in Isaiah," 2.

in Isa 49:6, He says, "It is too small a thing that You should be My Servant. To raise the tribes of Jacob, and to restore the preserved ones of Israel; I will also make you a light of the nations, so that My salvation may reach to the end of the earth."

Third, the INE functions as the hermeneutical pattern in the New Testament. The reworking of the foundational salvation story of the Old Testament is the INE theme with which Isa 40–55 begins, ends, and structures Luke's work.[57] Simeon references the INE in Luke 2:25 when saying that the consolation of Israel had arrived. It continues with John the Baptist in Luke 3:4 citing Isa 40 to describe his baptism of repentance in the greater one (YHWH) to come. After the temptation in the wilderness which also had INE themes, Jesus quotes the INE in the synagogue of Nazareth and throughout his ministry.

The Design of the INE. Watts describes the INE as following a design that involves three stages:

> 1) YHWH's deliverance of his exiled people from the power of the nations and their idols; 2) the journey along the "Way" in which YHWH leads his people from their captivity among the nations; and 3) arrival in Jerusalem, the place of his presence, where YHWH is enthroned in a gloriously restored Zion.[58]

This provides a pattern for the Gospel of Mark. The INE is carried out through the suffering and death of Jesus.

The Restoration of the People of God. Pao discerns six key themes related to the restoration of Israel.[59] We will summarize them here:

1. In Isaiah there is a concern for the twelve tribes of Israel (Isa 49:5–6) and the reunification of the divided kingdom (Isa 11:13; e.g., 7:1–9, 17; 9:9). The prologue of Isa 40–55 contains

---

57. Estelle, "Exodus Motif in Isaiah," 1.
58. Watts, *Isaiah's New Exodus in Mark*, 135.
59. Pao, *Acts and the Isaianic New Exodus*, 123–42.

the declaration of YHWH: "'Comfort, O comfort my people', says your God" (40:1). In Isa 40:10, "Behold, the Lord God will come with might, with His arm ruling for Him. Behold, His reward is with Him, and His recompense before Him." The Jews expected two related events regarding the reconstitution of Israel, according to Pao.[60] First, the twelve tribes will come together as in days of old. Second, there will be only one kingdom (Isa 11). This is considered an act of re-creation by YHWH as Israel's creator (Isa 43:1, 15), potter (43:1; 44:2, 24; 45:9, 11), and maker (44:2; 51:13; 54:5).

2. The rhetorical context (purpose, audience, and focus) of Isaiah includes the ingathering of the exiles as part of the reunification of Israel. Explicit statements regarding the ingathering of the exiles can be found throughout Isa 40–55:

> Do not fear, for I am with you; I will bring your offspring from the east and gather you from the west. I will say to the north, "Give them up!" And to the south, "Do not hold them back. Bring my sons from afar, and my daughters from the ends of the earth. Everyone who is called by My name, and whom I have created for My glory, whom I have formed even whom I have made." (Isa 43:5–7)

3. Reconstituted Israel is known as "the community of the Spirit." It is the work and power of the Spirit that characterizes the restored remnant of Israel (Isa 44:1–5). In Isa 42:1, the Spirit is promised to the servant who will carry out the will of God.[61] There is a direct connection between the Holy Spirit and the beginning of the age of restoration (Isa 32:14–17). Pao connects the early Christian community in the book of Acts with the eschatological community of the Spirit portrayed in Isaiah. This is signaled by the insertion of the phrase "in the last days" (ἐν ταῖς ἐσχάταις ἡμέραις) from Isa 2:1 at the beginning of the quotation from Joel (Acts 2:17).

---

60. Pao, *Acts and the Isaianic New Exodus*, 112.
61. Pao, *Acts and the Isaianic New Exodus*, 116.

The possible connections between Pentecost and the Sinai tradition further highlight this event.[62]

Pao highlights the significance of the Holy Spirit and the restoration of Israel as fulfilled on the day of Pentecost by highlighting Isa 32:15 in comparison with Acts 3:19–21.[63] The restoration of Israel is a process that will reach its completion at the end of time. The "times of refreshing" and the "times of universal restoration" of Isaiah are related to the coming of an eschatological age. The expression "times of refreshing" can be shown to signify the outpouring of the Spirit. This further connects Pentecost with the restoration of Israel.

4. Restored Israel also evokes the memory of the kingdom of David. In the epilogue to Isa 40–55, the promise to David is evoked: "Incline your ear and come to Me. Listen, that you may live; And I will make an everlasting covenant with you, according to the faithful mercies shown to David" (Isa 55:3). Isaiah 9:6–7 anticipates a Davidic ruler in the eschatological kingdom. The glory will return to Israel.

5. The restoration of Israel presupposes repentance. The people were scattered in foreign lands because of sin. This is a recurring theme throughout Isaiah (43:24–25; 44:21–22; 50:1). In response to the salvific act of God in Isa 43:24–25 a call to return to the Lord is issued (44:21–22). Especially in the latter part of Isaiah, there is a sustained appeal for repentance (Isa 56–66).

6. The inclusion of the outcasts is also part of the restoration of Israel theme in Isaiah. Acts 8:26–40 is the episode of the Ethiopian eunuch. He was reading Isa 53:7, which Phillip interprets for him as speaking of the crucifixion of Jesus. Pao states that the "inclusion of the conversion story of a eunuch within the restoration program of Luke is best understood as a sign that points to the place of the outcast in the reconstituted

---

62. Park, *Pentecost and Sinai*, 176.
63. Pao, *Acts and the Isaianic New Exodus*, 132.

people of God."⁶⁴ He states that it recalls Isa 56:3–5, which is thematically tied with the INE program of Isa 40–55.

The Promises to Abraham. Rikk Watts argues for a parallel with Abraham and the INE from Isa 51:2–5.

> It is possible that the movement from Abraham and Sarah to offspring (v. 2), to the restoration of the land (v. 3), and then to justice for the nations (vv. 4–5) is intended not only to invoke Genesis 12:1–3 but also its progression: Abram leaves Ur/Haran (Gen 12:1; Isa 40–55 just happens to be about an exodus from the same general location), is promised that he will become a great nation and be blessed (v. 2a), and finally is declared to be a blessing for all peoples on the earth (vv. 2b–3).⁶⁵

The INE includes allusions beginning with Abraham and continuing through Israel's history. When surveying the promises that include a role for the nations, the promise given to Abraham in Gen 12:1–3 is central to the INE.

The promises to Abraham are tied into the INE through the restoration of Israel and the inclusion of the gentiles. Bernard Anderson lists the motifs from the history of Israel that Isa 40–55 (DI) interprets eschatologically.⁶⁶ The birth of Israel is traced back to Abraham whom, when he was but one, YHWH called out and blessed. "Look to Abraham your father, and to Sarah who gave birth to you in pain; When he was one, I called him, then I blessed him and multiplied him" (Isa 41:8; 51:1, 2). The blessings of Abraham would continue to his descendants (Isa 48:18–19). These blessings include land, the fertility of "barren" Israel, and the mediation of saving benefits to other nations (Isa 54:18–19; 42:6–7). The promise to restore Israel and the promise to Abraham to be a light to the nations tie together in Isaiah. Isaiah 49:5–6 states,

---

64. Pao, *Acts and the Isaianic New Exodus*, 141.
65. Watts, *Echoes from the Past*, 495.
66. Anderson, "Exodus Typology in Second Isaiah," 182.

> And now, says the Lord, who formed me from the womb to be His servant, to bring Jacob back to Him, so that Israel might be gathered to Him (For I am honored in the sight of the Lord, and my God is my strength). He says, "It is too small a thing that you should be My Servant, to raise up the tribes of Jacob, and to restore the preserved ones of Israel; I will also make you a light to the nations so that My salvation may reach to the end of the earth."

The Servant of the Lord had a twofold task directly tied to the promise of Abraham (Gen 12:3; 17:4–6). Exodus 7:6; 14:1; 19:5–6 reiterate this idea where the expression "treasured possession" refers to a special status which includes being a light to the nations. The twofold task was to "raise up the tribes of Jacob and to be a light to the nations."

Fusion of Mosaic and Davidic Traditions. Park concludes that the INE theme fuses Mosaic and Davidic traditions and enables Luke to present Jesus as "the Davidic Messiah who is also the prophet like Moses."[67] The restoration of Israel/Jacob in their ancestral home includes the expectation that the Davidic monarchy will be reestablished. Mark Strauss agrees,

> If the Isaianic new exodus is Luke's primary model, this would go far in explaining why Luke—though consciously redacting in favor of a new exodus motif—continues to present Jesus in terms which recall both the Davidic king and the Isaianic servant. The Isaianic eschatological deliverer is at the same time prophet (like Moses), Davidic king and suffering servant of YHWH.[68]

The new covenant accompanies the INE. Isaiah 55:3 says, "Incline your ear and come to Me. Listen, that you may live; And I will make an everlasting covenant with you, according to the faithful mercies shown to David" (e.g., Isa 54:10; 55:1, 2). Isaiah makes numerous references to the Davidic covenant (9:1–7; 11:4, 5; 16:5;

---

67. Park, *Pentecost and Sinai*, 181.
68. Strauss, *Davidic Messiah in Luke Acts*, 262.

37:32; 42:3,4; 53:2; 59:17; 63:1). Strauss notes that Isa 9:1–7 and 11:1–16 are closely related to the royal psalms since they speak in exalted language concerning a coming Davidic king.[69] Isaiah's image of a "shoot" or sprout from the stump of Jesse (11:1) became a favorite metaphor for the coming Davidic king.

Former Things and New Things. Bernard Anderson shows how in chapters 40–48, "Isaiah juxtaposes the first things and the new things. The following passages develop this theme: Isaiah 40:6–9; 41:21–29; 43:8–13; 43:14–21; 44:6–8; 45:20–21; 46:8–11; 48:3–8; 48:14–16."[70] What does he mean by "former things" and "new things"? "Isaiah knew a historical tradition which reached back before the patriarchal period to the Creation."[71] A common meaning exists between the old exodus and the new. This parallelism is not mere poetic analogy—it is an expression of the unity and continuity of history in YHWH's purposive and dynamic will. "Moreover, the Exodus is a guarantee that YHWH will redeem his people, for that event demonstrates that he has the wisdom and power to accomplish what he purposes."[72]

YHWH is the only Lord of history, for he accomplishes what he announces. Israel's redemption will surely come, for YHWH's historical purpose runs consistently from the remote past to the present and on to the future. From a standpoint of faith, a consistent purpose runs through history from first to last—undergirding the present with meaning.

The Way Typology. Bo H. Lim shows how "the way" typology is used in the exodus motif.[73] YHWH prepared a way through the wilderness and led his people toward their destination (Isa 11:16; 35:8–10; 40:3–5; 42:16; 43:19). The exodus motif is used in the

69. Strauss, *Davidic Messiah in Luke Acts*, 37.
70. Anderson, "Exodus Typology in Second Isaiah," 185.
71. Anderson, "Exodus Typology in Second Isaiah," 184.
72. Anderson, "Exodus Typology in Second Isaiah," 189.
73. Lim, *"Way of the Lord" in Isaiah*, 159.

INE. The same is true when introducing Jesus's ministry. The wilderness motif is prevalent in the Gospels when introducing the INE theme (i.e., John the Baptist, the temptation of Jesus). Along the way, he supplied his people with food and drink (Isa 41:17–20; 43:19–21; 49:10). He made water flow from the rock (Isa 48:21; e.g., Exod 17:2–7; Num 20:8). During the new exodus, YHWH will marvelously transform the wilderness (Isa 35:6–7; 49:9–11; 55:13).

Lim states, "Isaiah 40 announces that 'the way' has been inaugurated. In this chapter, the focus is on YHWH's coming in a theophany, not the return of the people. DI combines Israel's traditions of creation and exodus to produce a message of hope as well as repentance."[74] The way (ὁδός) functions as an important theme to define discipleship. Jesus not only teaches the "way of God" (12:14) but his disciples "follow in the way" (10:52). Luke uses Isa 40:3–5 in Luke 1:17, 76–79; 2:30–31; 3:3–6; and 9:52.

Pao ties the imagery of "the way" to the ingathering of the exiles.[75] Isaiah 35:8–10 and others form the central core of the INE theme in which the people of God are called out and reunite as a nation in the land. As in the Exodus story, the people will "go out" from the nations, and "the Lord will go before you, and the God of Israel will be your rear guard" (52:12). God who has "formed you (Israel) in the womb" (44:24) once again calls his people to come out to a new community to be his "witnesses."[76] Pao states the term "way" in Isa 40–55 "became a term that evoked the Exodus tradition and signaled the presence of the new salvific act of God." This suggests the Isaianic tradition functions as a hermeneutical principle for the narrative of Luke-Acts.[77]

Bo H. Lim describes the new exodus and the Way of the Lord (hereafter WOL/INE) as the same. He states that for half a century, the WOL/INE has been considered by scholars as the theme of Isa 40–55. He considers that the theme spans the whole book and that

---

74. Lim, *"Way of the Lord" in Isaiah*, 160.
75. Pao, *Acts and the Isaianic New Exodus*, 114.
76. Pao, *Acts and the Isaianic New Exodus*, 114.
77. Pao, *Acts and the Isaianic New Exodus*, 66.

it is not brought out in studies that divide Isaiah. The theme of the WOL/INE unifies the book of Isaiah.[78]

Lim lists the WOL/INE texts in Isa 40–55:

40:3–11 The highway in the wilderness
41:17–20 The transformation of the wilderness
42:14–17 YHWH leads his people in a way they know not
43:1–7 Passing through the waters and the fire
43:14–31 A way in the wilderness
44:1–5 Drying of the water deep
48:20–21 Exodus from Babylon
49:8–12 The new entry into the Promised Land
50:2 Power to deliver
51:9–10 New victory at sea
52:11–12 The new exodus
55:12–13 Israel shall go out in joy and peace.[79]

The INE describes much more than the return from Babylon. Even though people returned to Jerusalem, the state of subjugation by a foreign government remained. Preparing the WOL as John the Baptist preached was not related to a roadway but rather to humility and repentance required in the presence of the Lord. "The WOL is both a historical and eschatological reality, and participation in this act of salvation requires moral and cultic purity."[80]

Even though Cyrus is portrayed as YHWH's representative in liberating the people of Israel, he only partially fulfills the redemptive promises of Isa 40–55. Chapter 42 announces the coming of the anointed Redeemer. The continuance of the WOL theme even after Israel has returned to Jerusalem from Babylon is indicative of a future eschatological fulfillment.

Pao shows that the "way" terminology is an identity claim in Acts for the true Israel.[81] The term appears in Acts 9:2; 19:9, 23; 22:4; and 24:14, 22. Notably, early Christian literature contains no clear parallel to the "way" apart from Acts and the writings

---

78. Lim, *"Way of the Lord" in Isaiah*, 2.
79. Lim, *"Way of the Lord" in Isaiah*, 47.
80. Lim, *"Way of the Lord" in Isaiah*, 168.
81. Pao, *Acts and the Isaianic New Exodus*, 59.

dependent on it. Pao unpacks the rhetorical role of the "way" terminology in the narrative of Acts. He states, "In examining the literary context of these passages, I will show that the way-terminology is used in polemical contexts where the identity of the 'true' people of God is at stake. The way terminology is therefore utilized in establishing the church as the true heir of ancient traditions of Israel."[82]

There is a definite connection with the thematic framework of Isa 40:3–5. "It is the formative power of the foundation story of Israel that ties the Isaianic program and the narrative of Acts together for both are concerned with the issue of continuity and discontinuity."[83]

Gospel Motif in Isaiah. Isaiah references the "gospel" motif (40:1–11; 41:21–29; 52:7–12; 60:1–11; 61:1–11). Isaiah 40:1–11 begins with the verb phrase "comfort, comfort my people" (παρακαλεῖτε, παρακαλεῖτε μου τὸν λαόν—LXX; e.g., Isa 51:9). This is the same word mentioned by Luke to express what Simeon was waiting for during the time that Jesus was born. Luke 2:25 says that he was waiting for the "consolation of Israel" (παράκλησιν τοῦ Ἰσραήλ), and it states that the Spirit was upon him (ἐπ' αὐτόν). Aker writes, "Isaiah 40:1–2 contains the significant text that sets forth the entire enterprise of new exodus deliverance in terms of 'comfort' or 'consolation' (LXX *paraklesis*, paraclete)."[84]

Isaiah 40:3 has the call, "Voice of one calling in the desert, 'prepare the way of the Lord!'" This is the text of the message of John the Baptist in Luke 3:4–6 relating to the arrival of the salvation of Israel. There is a gospel message in Isa 40 as part of the new exodus motif. Craig Evans states, "The way of the Lord alludes to the way through the sea that God provided the fleeing

---

82. Pao, *Acts and the Isaianic New Exodus*, 60.
83. Pao, *Acts and the Isaianic New Exodus*, 69.
84. Aker, "Paraclete," loc. 7492.

Israelites."[85] This is a type of future deliverance (Exod 14-15; Isa 42:15; 43:16-17; 43:19; 51:10-11).

Watts states that εὐαγγέλιον appears to be dependent upon Old Testament concepts of which the exemplary specimens appear in Isaiah. He says that in the Hebrew Scriptures and the LXX, the theological use of the verbal form (εὐαγγελίζω) is prevalent.[86]

Isaiah refers to the "redeemed" (λελυτρωμένοις) in 51:10-11 which brings to mind the Song of Moses celebrating God's redemption of Israel (Exod 15:13). Λυτρόω means "free by paying a ransom, redeem."[87] It is used in Luke 1:68 in the prophecy of Zechariah, "Blessed be the Lord God of Israel, For He has visited us and accompanied redemption for His people" (e.g., Luke 24:21; Isa 44:22-24; Acts 7:35).

Isaiah 40-55 contains passages that expound on of the "good news" using terms that Luke uses in the NT such as εὐαγγελίζομαι and παράκλησις or variants thereof. All the passages translate "good tidings."[88] Evans makes note that significantly, in all five passages, YHWH is himself the subject of the good tidings. He states, "The theocentric dimension of these oracles is primary. It is the presence and reign of God that constitute the good tidings or gospel."[89] These are passages in Isa 40-55 that mention "good news":

1. Isaiah 40:9: ἐπ' ὄρος ὑψηλὸν ἀνάβηθι, ὁ εὐαγγελιζόμενος Σιων, ὕψωσον τῇ ἰσχύι τὴν φωνήν σου, ὁ εὐαγγελιζόμενος Ιερουσαλημ, ὑψώσατε, μὴ φοβεῖσθε, εἰπὸν ταῖς πόλεσιν Ιουδα Ἰδοὺ ὁ θεὸς ὑμῶν—"Go up on a high mountain, O bringer of good news to Zion; lift up your voice with strength, o bringer of good tidings to Jerusalem! Lift up do not fear! Say to the cities of Juda, Look; your God!" (LES).

---

85. Evans, "From Gospel to Gospel," 654.
86. Watts, *Echoes from the Past*, 96.
87. BDAG 484.
88. Strong, *New Strong's Concise Dictionary*, Heb. *Basar*, no. 1319.
89. Evans, "From Gospel to Gospel," 656.

2. Isaiah 41:27: ἀρχὴν Σιων δώσω καὶ Ιερουσαλημ παρακαλέσω εἰς ὁδόν—"I will give dominion to Zion, and I will comfort Jerusalem" (LES).

3. Isaiah 52:7: ὡς ὥρα ἐπὶ τῶν ὀρέων, ὡς πόδες εὐαγγελιζομένου ἀκοὴν εἰρήνης, ὡς εὐαγγελιζόμενος ἀγαθά, ὅτι ἀκουστὴν ποιήσω τὴν σωτηρίαν σου λέγων Σιων βασιλεύσει σου ὁ θεός—"As an hour upon the mountains, as the feet of one who brings the good news of peace, as the one who brings the good news of good things; for I will make your salvation heard, saying 'O Zion, your God will reign'" (LES).

4. Isaiah 60:6: ἀγέλαι καμήλων, καὶ καλύψουσίν σε κάμηλοι Μαδιαμ καὶ Γαιφα, πάντες ἐκ Σαβα ἥξουσιν φέροντες χρυσίον καὶ λίβανον οἴσουσιν καὶ τὸ σωτήριον κυρίου εὐαγγελιοῦνται— "herds of camels, and camels of Midian and of Ephah will cover you. Everyone from Sheba will come bearing gold, and they will carry frankincense and proclaim the salvation of the Lord" (LES).

5. Isaiah 61:1, 2: Πνεῦμα κυρίου ἐπ' ἐμέ, οὗ εἵνεκεν ἔχρισέν με, εὐαγγελίσασθαι πτωχοῖς ἀπέσταλκέν με, ἰάσασθαι τοὺς συντετριμμένους τῇ καρδίᾳ, κηρύξαι αἰχμαλώτοις ἄφεσιν καὶ τυφλοῖς ἀνάβλεψιν καλέσαι δεκτον εν αυτὸν Κυρίου καὶ ἡμέραν ανταποδόσεως—"The Spirit of the Lord is upon me, on account of which he has anointed me; he has sent me to bring good news to the poor, to heal those who are crushed in heart, to announce release to the captives and recovery of sight to the blind, to proclaim the acceptable year of the Lord and the day of repayment" (LES).

Besides the presence and reign of God, Isaiah's good tidings also entail healing and restoration. According to Isa 61:1–3, the anointed herald is to bind up the brokenhearted and to open the eyes of the blind. This language (Isa 35) also speaks of the wilderness (v. 1), of seeing the glory of YHWH (v. 3), of a highway that will be called holy way (v. 8), and of the return of the ransomed of YHWH (v. 10).[90]

Westermann surveys Isaiah's salvation message as being distinct from all other Old Testament messages of salvation in that its essence is about the proclamation of an event regarded as having already come about.[91] Isaiah proclaims that the change from judgment to salvation was already an accomplished fact. The prologue itself starts this way, "'Comfort, O comfort My people,' says your God. 'Speak kindly to Jerusalem; And call out to her, that her warfare has ended, that her iniquity has been removed, that she has received of the Lord's hand double for all her sins'" (Isa 40:1–2). Isaiah 44:23 also speaks of Israel's redemption as an accomplished event.

Joy in Isaiah. Another characteristic of Isaiah's gospel is joy. Isaiah commands to be joyful in several places (40:9; 41:16; 51:11; 52:8, 9; 54:1; 55:1). The commands to rejoice apply to all the inhabitants, wild beasts of the desert, heaven and earth, and mountains and trees (42:10, 11; 43:20; 44:23; 49:13; 55:12). Isaiah does more than command joy. Its message is such that it has joy as its inevitable response.[92]

Westermann considers that the songs of praise or cries of exultation (42:10–13; 44:23; 45:8; 48:20; 49:13; 51:3; 52:9; 54:1–2) are in response to a call for decision.[93] The nature of a gospel of salvation rules out any idea of avoiding commitment. Existential acceptance of his message consists of the immediate raising of shouts of praise—an indication of faith. Isaiah's song of praise shows that in the Old Testament praise may take the place of what the New Testament calls faith.

Luke adds a note that Matthew and Mark do not mention. Luke mentions that as the formerly paralyzed man walks home, he

---

90. Evans, "From Gospel to Gospel," 656.
91. Westermann, *Isaiah 40–66*, 31–46.
92. Westermann, *Isaiah 40–66*, 12.
93. Westermann, *Isaiah 40–66*, 19.

was praising God. Luke records the gratitude and joy that comes with the saving action of God (e.g., Luke 2:20; 4:15; 5:26; 7:16; 13:13; 17:15; 18:43; 23:47; Acts 4:21; 11:15–18; 21:20). Joy is a characteristic mentioned in both Isaiah and Luke.

Repentance in Isaiah. Healing and restoration in Isaiah presuppose repentance. Evans describes the ministry of restoration of the INE and compares it to Isa 35:1–10, which includes many WOL/INE themes (wilderness, glory of the Lord, the "way" terminology, and the return of the "ransomed of the Lord"). "Behold our God!" (Isa 35:4) is like the proclamation in 40:9. Evans states it thus:

> It will be a time when the "eyes of the blind will be opened, and the ears of the deaf unstopped; then will the lame man leap like a hart, and the tongue of the dumb sing for joy" (vv. 5–6). Repentance is a prerequisite, however, for the realization of the good tidings. Throughout the second half of Isaiah we hear calls for a return (ἐπιστρέφω) to God (Isa. 44:22, 46:8); "let the wicked forsake his way, and the unrighteous man his thoughts; let him return, to YHWH, that he may have mercy on him, and to our God, for he will abundantly pardon" (55:7); "and he will come to Zion as Redeemer, to those in Jacob who turn from transgression, says YHWH" (59:20). Forgiveness, understood in the second half of Isaiah in terms of liberation, is the result: "to let the oppressed go free" (58:6); "to proclaim liberty to captives" (Isa 61:1–3). In the LXX ἄφεσις ("forgiveness") translates these terms.[94]

Roberts sustains that the holiness of God is an overarching theme of Isaiah. He notes that this holiness produced repentance in Isaiah. He sees an ethical element in Isaiah's understanding of YHWH's holiness.[95] Fellowship with God demands that one be purged of one's sins. Even though YHWH's glory fills the whole earth, he is, nonetheless, the Holy One of Israel.

---

94. Evans, "From Gospel to Gospel," 657.
95. Roberts, "Isaiah in Old Testament Theology," loc. 1008.

In the second part of Isaiah, there is still an emphasis on Israel's trouble being due to the sins of her people (42:24–25). They deserved their dire straits. Isaiah 40–55 ends with an admonition to the wicked to forsake wickedness and turn to YHWH while he may still be found (55:6–7). The third section of Isaiah emphasizes true religion and a turn to God. It denounces as vain any attempt to win God's favor based on cultic performances that leave the rest of life unaffected (Isa 58:3–5).[96] God's fiery judgment is mentioned as a future possibility (65:11–15; 66:15–17).

In the third part, Isaiah speaks of preparing a way in a moral sense. He claims that the Holy One of Israel lives not only in the heights but also with the contrite heart.

> And it shall be said, "Build up, build up, prepare the way. Remove every obstacle out of the way of my people." For thus says the high and exalted One, who lives forever, whose name is Holy. "I dwell on a high and holy place, and also with the contrite and lowly of spirit to revive the spirit of the lowly and to revive the heart of the contrite." (Isa 57:14)

Servant Songs. Reed Lessing explains the "servant songs" of Isa 40–55.[97] Isaiah contains four servant songs (42:1–4; 49:1–6; 50:4–9; 52:13—53:12). The first servant song in Isa 42:1–4 initially refers to the nation of Israel. How can this be since Matthew quotes the song to describe Christ's ministry?[98] Although at the outset this song applies to the nation of Israel, its fulfillment is in Jesus. Lessing shows his interpretation of the first song by considering the narrative flow of Isa 41–48. The first use of "servant" is in 41:8 and refers to the nation of Israel/Jacob. After 42:1–9, YHWH calls the same servant "blind and deaf" (42:18–20). Because the

---

96. Roberts, "Isaiah in Old Testament Theology," loc. 1050.
97. Lessing, "Isaiah's Servant," 132.
98. Matt 12:18–21.

servant/nation is idolatrous (42:17; 44:9-20), she is unable to be a "covenant for the people and a light for the nations" (42:6).[99]

The servant in Isa 49-55 is a replacement for the nation of Israel/Jacob. This is the suffering servant who speaks for the first time in 48:16, "And now the Lord God has sent Me, and His Spirit." The connection between 48:16 and 49:1-6, and 50:4-9 is clear. The theme of the Spirit is the same as in 42:1. Both servant Israel and the suffering servant are directed by YHWH's Spirit. Idolatry defeats the first servant. The victory of the second brings light and life to the world. Servant songs two, three, and four all point to Jesus.

Visions of Peace. Isaiah 55:1-13 is the first of three visions of peace in Isa 40-66. It begins by inviting those who are thirsty and without money to come and eat. Isaiah links the invitation to life, to the everlasting covenant. The vision concludes with imagery of peace that results in rejoicing and gladness. The mountains and the hills sing. The trees break into applause. This imagery of life and peace provides a sign that the covenant will be long-lasting.

The second vision of peace is in Isa 60:17-22. There is a contrast in present conditions with those to come. This appears in the list of building materials for the new Jerusalem. New materials such as gold, silver, bronze, and iron will replace bronze, iron, wood, and stones used in Solomon's city. There will be peace, and light will come from God and not from the sun and moon. The final vision of peace in Isaiah comes in Isa 65:17-25. Something new is on the horizon. There will be no crying or weeping and food and other resources will be plentiful, and life will be long.[100]

A Light to the Nations. Ronald E. Clements seeks to determine whether there is an underlying theme to Isaiah. He refers to the contention that the book is composed of at least three separate

---
99. Lessing, "Isaiah's Servant," 131.
100. Leiter, "Visions of Peace in Isaiah," 244-52.

books as being a hindrance to considering a common theme underlying the whole. "The book of Isaiah contains a unified purpose related to Jerusalem—Zion, the central role of the royal dynasty of David, and to the leadership that Israel is to assume among the nations."[101]

Within the theme of being a light to the nations, the images of "remnant" and "servant" prevail. These images were to become central to the New Testament's reinterpretation of Israel as an ἐκκλησία—a church.[102] These have become key Christian hermeneutical guidelines for the New Testament interpretation of the Bible as a canonical whole. These terms are necessary to understand both disaster and deliverance within the divine scheme of things. Clements states it well, "Israel's relationship to the Lord God is seen as established through worship and total spiritual loyalty, making the language of servanthood and remnant into primary terms through which the bond between God and the nation is given expression."[103]

The metaphor of light to the nations as a metaphor for salvation is prevalent in Isaiah. Clements notes that the noun "light" (LXX φῶς, Heb. 'or) occurs no less than twenty-two times in Isaiah. Clements notes that in Isa 10:17 the metaphor of light, implying salvation, could also imply "fire" bringing judgment.[104] Ambiguity is deliberately employed as in the metaphor "remnant" to show that judgment and salvation can be understood together. The actions that bring salvation imply judgment for others. The imagery of light as a metaphor of salvation provides an important counterpart to the imagery of blindness that occupies a central place in Isaianic theology.

First, it is the light that removes Israel's blindness. This is evident in the introduction of the theme as a metaphor of salvation in Isa 9:2, "The people who walk in darkness will see a great light." Israel's spiritual darkness highlights the coming of the new

101. Clements, "Light to the Nations," 60.
102. Clements, "Light to the Nations," 61.
103. Clements, "Light to the Nations," 61.
104. Clements, "Light to the Nations," 69.

light that shall shine and take the form of a new deliverer-king (Isa 9:2–7). This is clear in Isa 10:17, "And the light of Israel will become a fire and his Holy One a flame, and it will burn and devour his thorns and his briars in a single day." Clements identifies three key passages in which "the metaphor of light as a sign of salvation occurs in Isaiah (9:2; 42:6; 60:1–3)."[105] These unite the theme of the three-fold division of Isaiah.

Parental Imagery. Sarah Dille explores five units of DI searching for metaphors and their interactions with their literary and cultural contexts. The five units in DI that she examines are Isa 42:8–17; 43:1–7; 45:9–13; 49:13–21; and 50:1–3. She attempts to demonstrate how these passages interact using the images of father and mother for YHWH.[106] These two images further interact with the images of a warrior, redeeming kinsman, artisan, and the city as a woman, wife, and mother. The passages and the father/mother images are listed below:

1. In Isa 42:8–17, the image of God as a woman in labor interacts with that of the divine warrior. This section highlights "crying out," anguish, courage, danger, inevitability, the hope of deliverance from death, life, and the literary convention of one facing a siege reacting "like a woman in labor."

2. In Isa 43:1–7 God as father interacts with God as the kinsman who redeems his kin from slavery. This interaction highlights honor, identity, deliverance, protection, and the exodus tradition.

3. In Isa 45:9–13, the image of the begetting father and the laboring mother interact with the image of the artisan shaping the clay. The dominant area of coherence is the concept of creator.

4. In Isa 49:13–26, the image of Zion as a mother bereaved of her children elicits the image of God as a nursing mother (who

---

105. Clements, "Light to the Nations," 68.
106. Dille, *Mixing Metaphors*, 2.

does not forget her children). Zion's forgetting contrasts with YHWH's remembrance.

5. In Isa 50:1–3, the image of God as a father is prompted by the interaction of the images of God as a husband and Zion as a mother. YHWH is the husband of Zion whose children have been sold. Where more than one metaphor is used in a section, the overlapping meaning is surveyed.[107]

Covenant. Ulrich F. Berges emphasizes the covenant in Isaiah.[108] Isaiah 24 and 54:9 both mention the Noahic covenant. The allusions to the covenant with Noah are clear. After the flood YHWH commits himself to remember the eternal covenant (Gen 9:16). Punishment is different from not keeping the covenant. "The reckoning of those on earth who break the covenant is like the pickings of the olive harvest: only very few escape the beating strokes and avoid the olive press" (Isa 24:12–13). In the background of the flood narrative in which only Noah and those with him survived (Gen 7:23), only the remnant is clearly in view.

There is a similarity between the covenant with Noah and that with Zion. As the earth will never again experience a flood, Zion will no longer suffer disgrace and shame; though mountains and hills may shake, "my grace will not depart from you; my covenant of peace shall not be moved, says YHWH, who has compassion on you." As YHWH gave the oath of an eternal covenant after the flood (Gen 9:16) never again to destroy the earth by flood, he now swears to his bride Zion after the exile never to be angry with her (Isa 54:9).

The Davidic covenant is mentioned also in Isa 55:3. With the mention of the nations in Isa 55:4, there is an emphasis on a three-way relationship instead of just the two-way relationship between YHWH and Israel. The circumstances of salvation confirmed by an oath from YHWH himself is the theme of 54:11–17. Zion shall

---

107. Dille, *Mixing Metaphors*, 2–3.
108. Berges, *Book of Isaiah*, 315.

be rebuilt from the foundations up. Isaiah 55:1–5 is an invitation to participate in the new covenant community; all who thirst are invited to come to the waters and feast. All who come to the life-giving source of Zion, YHWH will enter an "eternal covenant" with them—like the steadfast, sure love for David. This is understood concerning restored Israel that is created in the form of the church and "filled" with the Holy Spirit.

The first servant song of Isa 42:1–6 states, "I will appoint you as a covenant to the people, as a light to the nations, to open blind eyes, to bring out prisoners from the dungeon, and those who dwell in darkness from the prison." Bruce asserts that this passage is quoted in its entirety in Matt 12:18–21, which sees a definite fulfillment in the ministry of Christ. Bruce notes that the servant is publicly designated and acknowledged by God; is granted the permanent indwelling of the Spirit of God; and is to exercise a worldwide mission.[109]

Ruthven relates Isa 59:19–21 to Acts chapter 2 showing that the coming of the Spirit is the promised new covenant. He explains the structure of Acts contending that the Pentecost phenomena correspond more closely with Isaiah than with Sinai as Park and others claim.[110] There is a closer parallel with the language of Isa 59 than with the Sinai event. Isaiah 50:21 is clear in relating it with the covenant. The INE combines Abrahamic, Mosaic, and Davidic themes.

In the time of Jesus, the Jews related the Feast of Pentecost to the feast of covenant renewal. This would be true of the Qumran community also. In rabbinic Judaism, the giving of the law became associated with Pentecost; however, the rabbinic traditions associated with Pentecost developed more fully after the times of the early church. Only the feast of covenant renewal was present in pre-Christian Judaism. Moisés Silva states that the significance of Pentecost for Luke is based on the fulfillment of the divine promise and thus—the covenant.[111]

109. Bruce, *International Bible Commentary*, 749.
110. Ruthven, "This Is My Covenant with Them (Part I)," 33.
111. Silva, "πεντηκοστή," 710.

VanderKam shows that Luke was influenced by Jewish traditions about Sinai and the Festival of Weeks.[112] Park maintains that the Sinai parallel was arrived at by Luke solely based on the Old Testament Scriptures. This may not be relevant for it is likely that Luke never read Jubilees or the Dead Sea scrolls or Hebrew to any appreciable degree.

Park argues that the ascension and Pentecost narrative draws on the Sinai event and that Luke consciously draws a parallel between these events and Moses's ascent of Mount Sinai during the Festival of Weeks. He sees a parallel between Moses ascending and returning with the law and Jesus ascending and sending the Spirit at Pentecost in Jerusalem.[113] Park maintains that Luke did not need to make a connection between the book of Jubilees or the Dead Sea scrolls to come to this conclusion. He uses the INE theme found in Luke-Acts to show how Moses-typology was consciously used by Luke.[114] Central to the exodus account is the giving of the law on Mount Sinai.

The Word of God. Pao considers the subject of the "word of God" as key. He says that the word is "the powerful agent that accomplishes the program of the new exodus." He states that the "word is the main character of the book of Acts."[115] Isaiah 40:6–8 speaks of the word of God,

> A voice says, "Call out." Then He answered, "What shall I call out?" All flesh is grass, and all its loveliness is like the flower of the field. The grass withers, the flower fades, When the breath of the Lord blows upon it; surely the people are grass. The grass withers, the flower fades, But the word of our God stands forever.

Isaiah 40–55 contains significant passages concerning the word of God. Isaiah 55:10–11 is an important one:

112. VanderKam, "Covenant and Pentecost," 239.
113. Park, *Pentecost and Sinai*, 177.
114. Park, *Pentecost and Sinai*, 179.
115. Pao, *Acts and the Isaianic New Exodus*, 150.

> For as the rain and the snow come down from heaven, and do not return there without watering the earth, and making it bear and sprout, and furnishing seed to the sower and bread to the eater; so shall My word be which goes forth from My mouth; it shall not return to me empty, without accomplishing what I desire, and without succeeding in the matter for which I sent it.

Since Luke follows the INE closely, Pao argues that the word of God should be understood as the main character in the narrative of Acts (e.g., Acts 19:20).

Pao argues that the word of God throughout Acts in the travel narratives and summary statements concerning the growth of the word needs to be understood within the paradigm of the INE. "With the development of the narrative, the word becomes the powerful force that can conquer the world.... It is the powerful agent that accomplishes the program of the new exodus."[116] Pao traces the "word" throughout Acts (4:4; 4:29; 6:2–4; 8:1–3, 4, 25; 10:36; 11:1, 19; 12:3; 13:5, 12, 26, 42–44, 46, 48; 13:3; 14:25; 15:35, 36; 16:1–5, 6, 32; 17:11, 13; 18:5, 11, 19; 19:10, 20; 20:1–12, 32; 28:31). By surveying the occurrences of the word throughout, Pao shows that

1. The central character of the travel narrative is the word of God;
2. the word prevails in opposition;
3. the word's journey is linear. Although the "ministers of the word may travel in circular journeys, the word itself travels from Jerusalem to the ends of the earth without returning to the same city twice."[117]

The power of the word is explained by Pao by the word "hypostatization." He concludes thus by the statements that refer to the growth of the word:

---

116. Pao, *Acts and the Isaianic New Exodus*, 150.
117. Pao, *Acts and the Isaianic New Exodus*, 156.

1. Acts 6:7a. Καὶ ὁ λόγος τοῦ θεοῦ ηὔξανεν—"and the word of God was growing."
2. Acts 12:24. Ὁ δὲ λόγος τοῦ θεοῦ ηὔξανεν καὶ ἐπληθύνετο—"but the word of God was growing and was multiplying."
3. Acts 19:20. Οὕτως κατὰ κράτος τοῦ κυρίου ὁ λόγος ηὔξανεν καὶ ἴσχυεν—"so with the power of the Lord, the word was growing and strengthening."

Pao notes the imperfect of αὐξάνω in all three cases. He argues that in Lukan writings, this verb is used only regarding living matters (i.e., growth of Jesus and John the Baptist—Luke 1:80; 2:20). The closest indication that Luke presents the word as an independent being is found in Acts 13:48 when the gentiles who while hearing[118] were gladdened and "praised the word of the Lord and believed as many were appointed into eternal life"—ἀκούοντα δὲ τὰ ἔθνη ἔχαιρον καὶ ἐδόξαζον τὸν λόγον τοῦ κυρίου καὶ ἐπίστευσαν ὅσοι ἦσαν τεταγμένοι εἰς ζωὴν αἰώνιον. Pao notes that in Lukan writings the object of δοξάζω is always either God or Jesus. The only exception is Acts 13:48 where the word is the object.[119]

Pao discusses the unique conception in the INE of the word as the creative agent that accomplishes the divine will. In Isa 9:7 (8), the word (Heb. *davar*) is being sent as an instrument of the judgment of God. The Hebrew has "the Lord sent a word" against Jacob, whereas the LXX has θάνατος (death) that the Lord sent against Israel. The emphasis is on the power of the word in itself, not the content. In the prologue to Isa 40–55, it is declared the word of God will stand forever (Heb. *davar*). In the LXX it says, "the word of our God remains forever."[120] The word is an INE theme. Pao notes that the "breath of the Lord" and the "word of our God" become identical phrases that point to God's superior power over humanity.[121]

---

118. Present active participle masculine accusative singular—action simultaneous to the main verb.
119. Pao, *Acts and the Isaianic New Exodus*, 160.
120. τὸ δὲ ῥῆμα τοῦ θεοῦ ἡμῶν μένει εἰς τὸν αἰῶνα.
121. Pao, *Acts and the Isaianic New Exodus*, 165.

Signs and Wonders. When John the Baptist sent his messengers to ask if Jesus was the one or he should wait for another, Jesus supplied a recognizable list to John. Luke 7:21–3 says,

> At that very time He cured many people of diseases and affliction and evil spirits, and He gave sight to many who were blind. And he answered and said to them, "Go and report to John what you have seen and heard: the blind receive sight, the lame walk, the lepers are cleansed, and the deaf hear, the dead are raised up, the poor have the gospel preached to them. Blessed is he who does not take offense at Me."

Isaiah 61:1–2 says,

> The Spirit of the Lord God is upon me because the Lord has anointed me to bring good news to the afflicted; He has sent me to bind up the brokenhearted, to proclaim liberty to captives, and freedom to prisoners; to proclaim the favorable year of the Lord, and the day of vengeance of our God; to comfort all who mourn; to grant those who mourn in Zion, giving them a garland instead of ashes, the oil of gladness instead of mourning, the mantle of praise instead of a spirit of fainting.

The INE is mentioned throughout Isaiah and the Old Testament.

Table 2 displays the characteristics of the INE that also form the narrative of Luke-Acts. Luke uses the INE theme to show that the life and ministry of Jesus and ongoing outpouring of the Spirit and miracles in Acts can be best explained to the Jews and the world by Isaiah's eschatolization of Israel's identity story explained in detail in the INE. Everything in the history of Israel points toward the overarching purpose of God as fulfilled by Jesus at Calvary and on the day of Pentecost.

Table 2. The Isaianic New Exodus Themes

Theme	Scripture
(1) Restoration of the People of God	Isa 7:1–9, 17; 9:9; 11:13; 40:1–31; 43:5–7; Acts 1:8

(2) Recreation	Isa 43:1, 15 (Creator); 43:1; 44:2, 24; 45:9, 11 (Potter); 44:2; 51:13; 54:5 (Maker)
(3) Community of the Spirit	Isa 32:14–17; 42:1; 44:1–4; 50:21; 59:19–21; 61:1–2; Luke 4:18–19; Acts 2:17
(4) Davidic Covenant	Isa 9:6–7; Isa 40–55; 55:3
(5) Repentance	Isa 43:24–25; 44:21–22; 50:1
(6) Inclusion of the Outcasts	Isa 56:3–5; Acts 8:26–40
(7) Promises to the Fathers	Isa 41:8; 42:6–7; 48:18–19; 51:1; 54:18–19; 49:5–6
(8) Deliverance	Isa 40:5, 10; 42:16; 48:20; 49:9–10; 51:9; 52:10, 12
(9) Provision in the Wilderness	Isa 41:17–20; 43:19–21; 48:21; 49:9–10
(10) The Way of the Lord	Isa 11:16; 35:8–10; 40:3–5; 42:16; 43:19; Luke 1:17, 76–79; 2:30–31; 3:3–6; 9:52; Acts 9:2; 19:9, 23; 22:4; 24:14, 22
(11) New Covenant	Isa 55:3; 54:10; 55:1, 2
(12) Davidic and Mosaic Traditions	Isa 9:1–7; 11:4, 5; 16:5; 37:32; 42:3,4; 53:2; 59:17; 63:1
(13) Former and New Things	Isa 40:6–9; 41:21–29; 43:8–21; 44:6–8; 45:20–21; 46:8–11; 48:3–8; 48:14–16
(14) Gospel Motif	Isa 40:1–11; 41:21–29; 42:15; 43:16–17; 43:19; 44:22–24; 51:10–11; 52:7–12; 60:1–11; Luke 24:21; Acts 7:35
(15) Visions of Peace	Isa 55:1–13; 60:17–22; 65:17–25
(16) New Jerusalem	Isa 60:1–11
(17) Joy	Isa 40:9; 41:16; 42:10; 43:20; 44:23; 49:13; 51:11; 52:8; 52:9; 54:1; 55:1; 55:12
(18) Songs of Praise	Isa 42:10–13; 44:23; 45:8; 48:20; 49:13; 51:3; 52:9; 54:1
(19) Fire	Isa 1:24, 25; 6:6; 47:14; 65:11–15; 66:15–17

(20) Servant Songs	Isa 42:1–4; 49:1–6; 50:4–9; 52:13—53:12
(21) Light to the Nations	Isa 9:2; 10:17; 24:15; 31:9; 42:6; 47:14; 50:11; 60:1–3
(22) Parental Imagery	Isa 42:8–17; 43:1–7; 45:9–13; 49:13–21; 50:1–3
(23) Noahic Covenant	Gen 7:23; 9:16; 24:12–13; Isa 54:9
(24) Word of God	Isa 40:6–8; 55:10–11; Acts 4:4; 4:29; 6:2–4; 8:1–3, 4, 25; 10:36; 11:1, 19; 12:3; 13:5, 12, 26, 42–44, 46, 48; 13:3; 14:25; 15:35, 36; 16:1–5, 6, 32; 17:11, 13; 18:5, 11, 19; 19:10, 20; 20:1–12, 32; 28:31
(25) Signs and Wonders	Isa 61:1–2; Luke 7:21–23
(26) Vindication of YHWH	Isa 40:1—54:17

Kingdom of David

Scott Hahn argues that the kingdom of David informs Luke's presentation of Jesus as the Davidic king. He shows how all eight of the characteristics of the kingdom of David were present in Luke's portrayal of Jesus's person and mission.

1. The Davidic monarchy was founded upon a divine covenant (διαθήκη LXX).
2. The Davidic monarch was the Son of God (2 Sam 7:14).
3. The Davidic monarch was the "Christ," that is the "Messiah" or "Anointed One."
4. The Davidic monarchy was inextricably bound to Jerusalem (possession of David and his heirs, 2 Sam 5:9).
5. The Davidic monarchy was inextricably bound to the temple.
6. The Davidic monarch ruled over all twelve tribes. The reunification of Israel and Jacob was associated with the restoration of the Davidic monarchy.
7. The Davidic monarch ruled over an international empire.

8. The Davidic monarchy was to be everlasting (Pss 21:4; 72:5; 110:4).[122]

Hahn connects the Christology of Luke with the ecclesiology of Acts through Jesus's conferral of his Davidic kingdom at the institution narrative (Luke 22:19–20). Thus, the church is the restored Davidic kingdom spreading to the ends of the earth. The characteristics mentioned by Hahn are also included in the INE.

Bock notes a link to the Davidic promise:

> In Acts 2:30 there is a reference to God's promise to David about a descendant to be set on David's throne. The passage alluded to is Psalm 132:11 which is a commentary on the promise of 2 Samuel 7:8–16 (the Davidic Covenant) . . . . Peter argues that the ascension is an initial realization of a promise made to David.[123]

Psalm 132 ties Jesus's resurrection-ascension to messianic promise.

Mark Strauss mentions the fulfillment of the Davidic promise in Luke's birth narrative (1:26–38; 1:68–79; 2:1–20). Strauss examines the birth narrative to determine if it is programmatic for the whole of Luke-Acts. He lists the characteristic Lukan themes that appear in the birth narratives.[124] It is particularly Lukan that the new eschatological age is marked by joy and rejoicing and giving praise to God.[125] This theme is especially clear in the birth narrative. Repeatedly, Luke's Gospel stories conclude with the recipients of God's benefits praising and giving glory to God (Luke 5:25–26; 7:16; 13:13; 17:15, 18; 18:43). This theme continues in Acts (Acts 2:47) where praise accompanies both healings and salvation of the gentiles (Acts 3:8–9; 4:21; 11:18; 13:48; 21:20).

Typological parallels to the Old Testament abound in the nativity narratives. Care is taken to show that all is done according

---

122. Hahn, "Kingdom and Church," 300.

123. The Ps 132 citation links Peter's remarks about the fulfillment of Ps 16:8–11 in the resurrection and with Ps 110:1; Bock, *Theology of Luke and Acts*, 50.

124. Strauss, *Luke*, loc. 1224.

125. The INE commands to be joyful (Isa 40:9; 41:16; 51:11; 52:8; 52:9; 54:1; 55:1).

to the law of Moses. The purpose of the emphasis on the Old Testament and the faithful remnant confirmed by the Spirit "upon them" (ἐπ' αὐτόν) is the portrayal of a new eschatological era.

Significantly, Luke defines the promise primarily in terms of the Davidic promise.[126] In surveying the literature dealing with Luke's use of the Old Testament, different authors and positions surface (table 3). Though several subthemes can be identified in Luke-Acts that have merit, none cover all the text. The Sinai parallel of Park and VanderKam deals with Pentecost only. The kingdom of David motif is strong and is found throughout the text; also, many subjects surface like the way of the Lord, the inclusion of the outcasts (gentiles), suffering Messiah, and others that are not covered.

Given the data above, and the absence of several important themes in the identified motifs, the INE again emerges at the most comprehensive organizing principle. Just as Isaiah eschatologizes the Israel-identity story including Abrahamic, Mosaic, and Davidic traditions, Luke also transforms the INE theme to show the redemptive-historical context of his narrative. He does not extract parts of Isaiah to explain individual events. Isaiah is read in a new way as set in the co-text of Luke. Luke's narrated events are interpreted by the Isaianic vision of eschatological salvation.

Table 3. Luke's Use of the Old Testament

Theme	Academic Support	Description
Isaianic New Exodus	Pao, Kwon, Harris, Manek, Turner, Wilms, Wright	The INE is broad and includes the other themes presented.
Sinai Parallel	Park, VanderKam	The main emphasis is the parallel between Sinai and Pentecost.
Covenant Renewal	VanderKam, Park, Silva	Luke was influenced by Qumran and rabbinic traditions on Sinai and the Festival of Weeks.

126. Strauss, *Davidic Messiah in Luke Acts*, 86.

Kingdom of David	Hahn; Harris; O'Toole; Strauss; Wright, Bock	The kingdom of David informs Luke's presentation of Jesus as the Davidic king.
Promise Fulfillment	Carson, Liefeld, Bock, Keener, Kaiser, Squires, Kent, Kovacs, Sanders	For Luke, the ministry of Jesus, the Jesus movement, and the gentile mission are the fulfillment and continuation of the biblical story.

Subproblem Three: The Meaning of Baptism with the Holy Spirit

Holdcroft mentions four positions held by scholars regarding the baptism with the Holy Spirit:[127]

1. The believer's total experience with the Holy Spirit is his role to baptize him/her into the body of Christ. These scholars lack the experience of being filled with the Spirit,[128] and it becomes a bias or presupposition in their research. Their anti-Pentecostal studies are conditioned by an apologetic stance.[129]

2. A second group believes that Spirit baptism is initiatory (one with regeneration). There are subsequent fillings, but they are not called baptisms (Merrill Unger, Samuel Ridout, Kenneth Wuest, and many others).

3. A third position distinguishes between baptism by the Spirit into the body and baptism into the Spirit for service (Jasper Huffman, John R. Rice, R. A. Torrey, René Pache, Charles Finney).

---

127. Holdcroft, "Spirit Baptism," 30.

128. Leedy and Ormrod, *Practical Research*, argue for the validity of experience in qualitative research.

129. They are compelled to defend their lack of experience.

4. A fourth group includes Pentecostals who distinguish between the two baptisms, and the evidence for the second is speaking in other tongues (Ralph Riggs, E. S. Williams, P. C. Nelson, Myer Pearlman, Stanley Horton, French Arrington, Anthony Palma, and many others).
5. Finally, some believe in a baptism with the Spirit subsequent to conversion-initiation but without the initial evidence of speaking in tongues (F. F. Bosworth).

These different positions all differ from the present study in that they have not paid adequate attention to the INE as a theological explanation for Luke's work. The INE as paradigm for Luke makes Luke-Acts both didactic and historical narrative. In addition, the significance of Luke's emphasis on Jerusalem has not been explored in relation to the baptism with the Holy Spirit.

To defend the limited view of the baptism, recent Pentecostal studies have emphasized redaction criticism to the point of excluding Paul or saying that Luke was not acquainted with Paul's writings.[130] This is far from being clear or the result of consensus in theological circles. Mark Strauss states:

> The "we" sections of Acts reveal that Luke was with Paul on his second missionary journey (Acts 16:10–17), and then rejoined him at Philippi on Paul's return from his third journey (20:5–21:18). He stayed with Paul at Caesarea after his arrest and went with him to Rome (27:1–28:16).[131]

It complicates the doctrine of the inspiration of Scripture to say that Paul and Luke were not in agreement or that Luke simply was not acquainted with what Paul had to say. I. Howard Marshall states, "It would be more correct to say Luke describes the same basic Christian experience as Paul in different terminology."[132] Hans Conzelmann quotes Irenaeus asserting that Luke was "the follower of Paul."

---

130. Menzies and Menzies, *Spirit and Power*, 56.
131. Strauss, *Luke*, loc. 852.
132. Marshall, *Acts*, 26.

Irenaeus calls Luke a "follower and disciple of the apostles" (*sectator et discipulus apostolorum Adv. haer.* 3.10.1), "the follower of Paul" (ὁ ἀκόλουθος Παύλου *Adv. haer.* 3.1.1), and he says, "he was always with Paul and collaborated with him in (the work of) the gospel" (*inseparabilis fuit a Paulo et cooperarius eius in evangelio Adv. haer.* 3.14.1; a reference to Acts follows [15:39], particularly to the "we" in 16:10–11, 13; 20:6).[133]

His relationship with Paul accredits his work although he did not witness the resurrection.[134]

Irenaeus refutes the claim that Luke had a theology different than the one he had learned from Paul. This he said to prove that Paul did not have theology different than the other apostles. If it had been so, then Luke would have been evidence of it since Luke did not differ from Paul. He writes,

> Surely if Luke, who always preached in company with Paul, and is called by him "the beloved," and with him performed the work of an evangelist and was entrusted to hand down to us a Gospel, learned nothing different from him (Paul), as has been pointed out from his words, how can these men, who were never attached to Paul, boast that they have learned hidden and unspeakable mysteries.[135]

Scholars have identified a distinctive Lukan pneumatology different from Paul's.[136] Keener states that it appears that in both Luke's and Paul's theology, the "receiving of the Spirit"[137] is connected with conversion (Acts 2:38–39; 11:16–17; e.g., Luke 3:16); but Luke sometimes distinguishes regeneration from Spirit

---

133. Conzelmann, *Acts of the Apostles*, xxxii.

134. The "we" passages (Acts 16:10–17; 20:5–16; 21:1–18; and 27:1—28:16) show that he was an eyewitness traveling with the apostle Paul.

135. Conzelmann, *Acts of the Apostles*, xxxii, citing Irenaeus (*Adv haer* 3.14.1).

136. Stronstad, *Charismatic Theology of St. Luke*, 11.

137. The phrase "receiving the Spirit" is used in Acts 10:47; cf. 1:8; 2:33, 38; 8:15, 17; 19:2.

baptism chronologically (Acts 8:12–17; e.g., 2:4; 9:17; 19:5–6).[138] Keener argues that it is because "Luke stresses prophetic empowerment almost to the exclusion of other elements."[139] Luke's narratives usually reserve the language of "receiving the Spirit" for this focus on empowerment for mission. Keener argues that the "baptism with the Spirit" can be received at or after conversion.[140] Keener states:

> Just as Jesus's resurrection, exaltation to heaven, and gift of the Spirit are theologically united yet chronologically separated, believers receive access to the full work of the Spirit at conversion yet may experience aspects of the Spirit's empowerment subsequently (and not limited to a single occasion).[141]

Keener further states that:

> Those that emphasize the Bible's theological statements (such as Paul's comments) rather than narrative examples (such as stories in Acts) usually identify baptism with the Spirit with conversion to faith in Christ. Those who emphasize Acts over against Paul usually believe that baptism with the Spirit can occur after conversion.[142]

Marshall states that it would be correct to say that Luke describes the same basic Christian experience as Paul with different terminology.[143] The motifs of bringing deliverance and healing in fulfillment of Old Testament promises by an anointed person amid unbelief and opposition mark out how the story is to be understood. God acts throughout the narrative through agents. The Holy Spirit fills them so that they can convey God's messages (Luke 1:15, 67).

---

138. Keener, *Acts*, 164.
139. Keener, *Acts: Exegetical Commentary*, 1:681.
140. Keener, *Acts: Exegetical Commentary*, 1:681.
141. Keener, *Acts*, 164.
142. Keener, *Gift and the Giver*, 150.
143. Marshall, *New Testament Theology*, 129–206.

Menzies's argument is that Paul emphasized the Spirit's work for the entire Christian life while Luke emphasized Spirit's work mainly for prophetic inspiration which enables them to participate in the evangelistic enterprise of the church.[144] In an article for the *Journal of Pentecostal Theology*, Menzies states, "Luke's understanding of baptism in the Holy Spirit is different from that of Paul. It is missiological rather than soteriological in nature."[145] Menzies argues for Luke's emphasis on the "distinct and subsequent" from salvation position. He states, "We have seen that the concept of a Spirit-baptism distinct from conversion flows from Luke's theology of the Spirit . . . the Lucan gift of the Spirit should not—indeed, cannot—be equated with the Pauline gift of the Spirit which forms the climax of the conversion experience."[146] He claims there is a baptism with the Spirit that is a part of conversion and one subsequent to conversion.

Everything that Jesus did is through the power of the Spirit. Nothing happens in Scripture without the power of the Spirit. Turner explains the current within theological studies that the Spirit operates in the New Testament as the Spirit of prophecy. "What we are asked to believe is that Luke, a Hellenistic Christian writer of the last quarter of the first century, abandoned the very widespread Christian view that the Spirit was also directly connected with miracles—indisputably the view of Mark (3:22–30), Matthew (most notably at 12:15–18, 28, 31–32), and Paul (e.g., 1 Cor 12:9–10, 28), and that he opted instead for 'the typically Jewish concept of Spirit' (as 'the Spirit of Prophecy')."[147] The INE is characterized by the Spirit (Isa 42:1). Acts 1:8 states, "and you shall receive power when the Holy Spirit has come upon you."[148] The power and the Spirit go together with a simple reading of the text.

---

144. Menzies and Menzies, *Spirit and Power*, 192.

145. Menzies, "Luke's Understanding of Baptism: Pentecostal Dialogue," 86–101.

146. Menzies and Menzies, *Spirit and Power*, 194.

147. Turner, "Spirit and the Power," 129.

148. "ἀλλὰ λήμψεσθε δύναμιν ἐπελθόντος τοῦ ἁγίου πνεύματος ἐφ' ὑμᾶς."

Schweizer is an example of the Spirit of prophecy position. "In Luke, healings are not associated with the Spirit but with the name of Jesus, with faith in Jesus, with Jesus himself, with prayer, with bodily contact with apostles, and with the power of Jesus . . . above all, he gives power to preaching."[149] He suggests that the eschatological community is a community of prophets, and miracles and exorcisms are not through the power of the Spirit.[150]

Aker states, "My contention is that all Spirit operations are to be connected with Jesus and his work."[151] The union and lordship of Jesus and the believer channels the Spirit to work through him. "This wonderful relationship and union channel the Spirit to work through the whole person, using the person's redeemed wholeness while at the same time assisting and empowering him or her."[152] It could be said that virtually all of Jesus's works were done through the power of the Spirit. Thus, as a man, he depended on obedience, prayer, and complete submission to the Father—this brought forth the power of the Spirit to complete his task.

"'Not by might nor by power, but by My Spirit,' says the Lord of hosts" (Zech 4:6) is a verse that describes the work of the Holy Spirit in the Old Testament. Wilf Hildebrandt surveys the work of the Holy Spirit and rightly affirms the Spirit's presence starting from creation, through leadership, exodus, prophecy, and miracles. He states, "It is only God's word brought about by the Spirit that is effectual and able to supersede natural laws. . . . Jesus quotes Isaiah 61:1–2 to indicate that the miraculous results of his preaching are

---

149. Schweizer, "πνεῦμα," 408.

150. This poses a problem that is beyond the scope of this study. If Jesus performed miracles as the Son of God and not through the power of the Spirit, then his status as redeemer is compromised. In disagreement with those who insist that Jesus did not perform his miracles through the power of the Spirit, it is suggested that the whole teaching of being a member of the human race (temptation, High Priest discussion in Hebrews, kinsman redeemer, et al.) is a necessary part of the redemption process. Wilms, "Deuteronomic Traditions," 189, writes, "In Jesus, there is a fulfillment of obedience required of Israel, particularly in Deuteronomy, and in which Israel failed."

151. Aker, "Charismata," 65.

152. Aker, "Charismata," 65.

due to the anointing of the Spirit of the Lord (Luke 4:18–19). Jesus is aware that his power comes through the Spirit."[153] Words spoken by the prophets could come true and be fulfilled when the prophet was commissioned, inspired, motivated, and guided by the Spirit of God.

Keener takes the position that the timing of the baptism with the Holy Spirit is not the primary issue in Acts. He says that it was theologically ideal to receive the full impact of the Spirit at conversion and that whether people had the experience of empowerment was more important than when they received it. It is evidenced by an "overwhelming direction of the Spirit in uttering praise, prophecy, or witness."[154]

The noun form "baptism with the Spirit" is never used in the New Testament. In Acts 1:5 and 2:4, Luke uses both "filling" and the verbal form of Spirit baptism (Luke 1:15, 41, 67; Acts 2:4; 4:8, 31; 9:17; 13:9, 52). Baptism with/of the Spirit is compared with John's ministry. The Pentecostal view is that only "baptism" is compared. The INE promise (the context of Luke) defines Jesus's baptism with Spirit and fire as his entire work. James Dunn classifies the word "baptism" as a metaphor. The term "baptism" with the Holy Spirit and fire is used as a rhetorical device to bring out the comparison between John's ministry and that of Jesus.[155]

It is significant that Luke uses the phrase "they were filled" instead of "they were baptized." It is the word he used on the day of Pentecost (ἐπλήσθησαν). The term "baptism" refers to all the events of the INE (all of Jesus's ministry). The baptism with the Spirit and fire characterizes the whole of what Jesus said and did. Even though both words are metaphors, Luke's emphasis on the day of Pentecost is on the Spirit filling the church as a tabernacle among humankind. "Filling" also has the idea of completion.[156] The phrase "and fire" is no longer used to refer to the day of Pentecost. This suggests that Jesus's baptism with the Holy Spirit and

---

153. Hildebrandt, *Old Testament Theology of the Spirit*, 207.
154. Keener, *Gift and the Giver*, 168.
155. Dunn, *Baptism in the Holy Spirit*, loc. 739.
156. *DBL*, "πίμπλημι," 4398.

fire involved more than the coming of the Spirit in Acts 2:4. The metaphor of "fire" means judgment in Isaiah. Jesus's baptism with the Holy Spirit and fire involved salvation and anointing for ministry to the world and judgment upon those who reject the Son. This includes national Israel, and at the end of the age for those who reject God's redemption plan.

In explaining the Pentecost event, Peter cites Joel 2:28, 29 (3:1–5a LXX) as promise-fulfillment "this is that" *pesher* interpretation.[157] Significantly Joel contains common themes with the INE. In Joel 2:28 (3:1–5a LXX) it says,

> It will come about after this,
> That I will pour out My Spirit on all mankind
> And your sons and your daughters will prophesy,
> Your old men will have dreams,
> Your young men will see visions.

There is a common theme with Isa 32:15, 40:5, and 44:3 (also Ezek 39:29). Isaiah 32:15 says, "Until the Spirit is poured out upon us from on high . . . ." Isaiah 40:4 states, "Then the glory of the Lord will be revealed, and all flesh will see it together." Isaiah 44:3 says, "For I will pour out water on the thirsty land and streams on the dry ground; I will pour out My Spirit on your offspring, and My blessing on your descendants."

Pao links the "times of refreshing" of Acts 3:19, 20 to Isa 32:15.[158] The significance of Isa 32:15 is established by the phrase from the LXX "until a Spirit from on high is poured out on us" and its parallel to Luke 24:49, "so stay here in the city until you have been clothed with power from on high." This connection of the Spirit with the restoration of Israel (INE) can already be found in the quotation of Joel 2:28–32, a passage that describes the hope of restoration.

---

157. Pesher is an early Jewish principle of interpretation of the Scriptures which included contemporizing a prophecy, claiming to find a prophecy's fulfillment in events either in their day or in the immediate future. See Klein, Blomberg, and Hubbard, *Introduction to Biblical Interpretation*, 27–28.

158. Pao, *Acts and the Isaianic New Exodus*, 133.

Baptism belongs to the general group of practices connected with washing. Before the New Testament period, there was already a figurative use of the term. At first, it meant the provision of cultic purity, then in the NT, it was intended to express the complete renewal of human existence.[159] Significantly, John's baptism occurred in the Jordan River. Both the wilderness and the Jordan River were important symbols recalling the INE.

Webb lists six characteristics that are special to John's baptism:

1. "It was an expression of conversionary repentance—a reorientation of one's life returning to a relationship with God"[160] (βάπτισμα μετανοίας—used to describe John's baptism in Luke 3:3).

2. "For John and those being baptized, baptism was understood to mediate divine forgiveness" (Isa 55:7). The fact that John himself baptized others rather than the traditional self-baptism places him as a mediator of forgiveness. Webb states, "The mediatorial role of 'the baptizer' in performing baptism to mediate forgiveness is parallel to the mediatorial role of a priest in performing a sacrifice in the sacrificial system."[161] This parallel is significant since John came from a rural priestly family.

3. Baptism also purified from uncleanness. "In the Hebrew Bible and later Jewish thought, the use of immersion was primarily concerned with cleansing from uncleanness"[162] (Lev 15, 18; Num 19). John's baptism was related to cleansing following standard usage.

4. John's baptism foreshadowed the ministry of Jesus. "The imagery of 'Holy Spirit' and 'fire' removes the activities of the

---

159. Beasley-Murray, "Baptism," 466.
160. Webb, "Jesus's Baptism," 115.
161. Webb, "Jesus's Baptism," 116.
162. Webb, "Jesus's Baptism," 116.

expected figure from the realm of a literal water rite and yet the verb 'baptize' is used to characterize his activities."[163]

5. "John's baptism functioned as an initiatory rite into the 'true Israel.'" John announced that his baptism was necessary to be prepared for the coming of Jesus. "John's baptizing ministry, therefore, created a fundamental distinction between the repentant and the unrepentant, the prepared and the unprepared, those who would receive the expected figure's restoration and those who would be judged."[164] All of Israel was facing judgment and only the remnant would be saved. Baptism for repentance was the necessary rite to be included in the remnant. For John, only those who have repented and were baptized became true "children of Abraham."

6. John's baptism also may have been a declaration against the corruption of the temple establishment. If John's baptism offered forgiveness, then it was offered as an alternative to the sacrifices in the temple.[165]

The use of "baptize" in the story of Naaman may have been decisive for its later use to signify taking a ritual bath for cleansing. Immersion is taken for granted with the term. Examples of this are the prophecy that the Messiah will baptize with the Spirit and fire (Matt 3:11), baptism of the Israelites in the cloud and the sea (1 Cor 10:2), and the idea of Jesus's death as a baptism (Mark 10:38–39). John baptized for remission of sins in anticipation and prophetic announcement of the coming baptism with Spirit and fire. Isaiah 4:2–5 and Mal 3:1–6 refer to the messianic baptism as a time of judgment that would refine the people and fit them for the kingdom but "consume the wicked that they should not participate in it."[166]

John's baptism may best be viewed as a unique eschatological (i.e., end times) application, drawing conceptually from the

163. Webb, "Jesus's Baptism," 117.
164. Webb, "Jesus's Baptism," 118.
165. Webb, "Jesus's Baptism," 122.
166. Beasley-Murray, "Baptism," 466.

cleansing and initiatory rites of first-century Judaism. In the Old Testament and intertestamental Judaism fire is a common symbol for God's judgment. Isaiah 4:4 speaks in an eschatological context of a "spirit of judgment and a spirit of fire" that will cleanse the bloodstains from Jerusalem (e.g., Mal 3:2). Judgment as unquenchable fire appears in Isa 34:10; 66:24 (e.g., Luke 3:17). "He will baptize you with the Holy Spirit and with fire" (Luke 3:16) is a reference to Jesus's work both during his lifetime on earth and end-time judgment (Acts 10:42; Rev 15:4).

John's baptism was the royal and priestly anointing of Jesus.[167] It occurs with the same premises that the new exodus had begun; however, it clearly prophesies and prepares the way for what Jesus would do. It is important to note that priests, prophets, and kings would be anointed with oil in a public ceremony (Exod 28:41; 29:7; 1 Kgs 19:16; Judg 9:8; 1 Sam 16:12, 13; Ps 89:20). Jesus was anointed; however, it was directly with the Holy Spirit.

In almost identical wording, Luke and Matthew introduced Jesus's baptism in the form of a prophetic reproach that threatened Israel with judgment. Luke 3:16b–17 says, "He himself will baptize you in the Holy Spirit and fire. And His winnowing fork is in His hand to clean out His threshing-floor, and to gather the wheat into His barn, but he will burn the chaff with unquenchable fire."[168] Stanley Horton states, "When Jesus talks about fire, it is always the fire of judgment or destruction, especially of the hell (*gehenna*) of fire, which really refers to the lake of fire (Matt 5:22; 18:8, 9). The same thing is usually true in the Epistles (1 Cor 3:13; 2 Thess 1:8; Heb 12:29; 2 Pet 3:7)."[169]

Fire is also used on the day of Pentecost.[170] Seijin Park mentions several allusions to Sinai in the Pentecost narrative.[171] Max

---

167. Oepke, "βαπτίζω," 538.

168. Cf. 2 Thess 1:7–9; Isa 61:2; Mal 3:1–6; 4:1.

169. Horton, *What the Bible Says*, loc. 1474.

170. Fire, LXX πυρί=Heb. *esh*, appears both at Sinai, Exod 19:18, and Acts 2:3.

171. Park, *Pentecost and Sinai*, 209.

Turner summarizes the parallels between Sinai and Pentecost in the following manner:

> Both Philo and Luke (i) envisage a holy theophany before the assembled people of God; (ii) in each case we have to do with a redemptive-historical event on earth which is formative for that people of God, marking a real beginning of some kind—a mighty "sign" of mightier consequences.[172]

For the beginning of the new eschatological age, fire was a symbol of the coming of the Spirit as the dove was at Jesus's baptism. Horton states the tongues of fire preceded the Pentecostal baptism, however, and had nothing directly to do with it.[173] When the one hundred twenty were filled with the Holy Spirit, the sign was speaking in other tongues, not fire (Acts 2:4).

The baptism with the Spirit[174] is the crown of INE. It is part of the process of the restoration and unification of Israel and of the ongoing charge to be a blessing to the nations. Part of the process of evangelizing the world from the remnant of Israel to the gentiles—to the ends of the earth—is the filling with the Spirit. At this point, Luke describes the baptism as with the Spirit but does not mention "fire" as before. The next event was the "filling" with the Spirit on the day of Pentecost. Those of the remnant who receive Jesus as Lord are filled with the Spirit and those who reject his sacrifice on the cross are judged by their own rejection of Jesus as Lord.

A Pattern for All

Keener states that the promised gift of the Spirit in Acts 2:38–39, which refers to Jesus's followers' experience on Pentecost, is a paradigmatic expression of baptism with the Spirit—a pattern for all.[175]

---

172. Turner, *Power from on High*, 284–85.
173. Horton, *What the Bible Says*, loc. 1457.
174. ἐν πνεύματι τήν βαπτισθήσεσθε ἁγίῳ—Acts 1:5, NA^{28}.
175. Keener, *Acts: Exegetical Commentary*, 1:680.

Keener takes the issue of subsequence to be optional (sometimes in salvation, sometimes after). Keener further states that Luke does not explicitly associate the Spirit with regeneration but does so often with prophetic empowerment. He affirms that Luke makes clear that all Jesus's followers receive access to the sphere of the Spirit, yet he focuses on an empowerment dimension that sometimes appears subsequent in his narratives. He states, "Instead of reading his apparently ideal theological paradigm (2:38) into the narrative evidence, Luke allows for a diversity of pneumatic experience (8:12–17; 10:44–48; 19:5–6) and presumably invites his audience to show the same courtesy."[176]

Kingdom Restoration

When Jesus said that his disciples would be baptized with the Holy Spirit (Acts 1:5, 8), their first response was to suppose that the kingdom would be restored to Israel. There is a definite eschatological ushering into the new covenant/new exodus represented by the "baptism with the Spirit and fire." The kingdom was present where Jesus was—being welcomed into fellowship with Jesus was the same as being welcomed into the kingdom. He was the one around whom Israel was being reconstituted. As a prophet, he gathered followers that constituted the renewed Israel, the returned-from-exile people of YHWH. Jesus was the Messiah. The dawn of the era of salvation and the deliverance of the people of God and Jerusalem/Zion forms the principle underlying the INE.

Wright argues that Jesus was Israel in person, Israel's representative, the one in whom Israel's destiny was reaching its climax.[177] "Jesus, then, believed himself to be the focal point of the people of YHWH, the returned-from-exile people, the people of the renewed covenant, the people whose sins were now to be forgiven. He embodied what He announced. He was the true interpreter of the Torah; the true builder of the Temple; the true spokesperson

---

176. Keener, *Acts: Exegetical Commentary*, 1:681.
177. Wright, *Jesus and the Victory of God*, loc. 11224.

for Wisdom."[178] Something supernatural was invading history and it would never be the same again.

Keener states that the prophets frequently linked the coming of the Spirit with Israel's restoration (Isa 42:1; 44:3; 59:21; Ezek 36:24–28; 37:14; 39:29; Joel 2:28–31 [3:1–5a LXX]).[179] Therefore, any talk about the Spirit was eschatological in nature. For example, the program for Jesus's mission in the gospel appears in Luke 4:18–19, which quotes Isa 61:1–2, which refers to the restoration of Israel (Isa 40:1, 9; 41:13; 51:3, 12; 52:7, 9; 54:18; 60:6; 66:13). Luke allows for an interim period before Israel's final repentance and restoration. It is through the coming of the Spirit that Luke emphasizes realized eschatology.

Wright affirms the fulfillment of the INE through Jesus. According to Wright, Jesus taught and lived out the kingdom of God. Jesus believed that the real return from exile and the real return of YHWH to Zion were happening in and through his work. Israel's hope was related to land, family, Torah, and temple; Jesus offered fresh and positive alternatives to these. Wright states, "Jesus's mighty works of healing were to be understood symbolically as a fulfillment of the expectation in Isaiah 35:1–2, 5–6, 10. They spoke clearly as symbols of return and restoration, of the coming of YHWH to save and heal his people."[180]

Jesus did not have random teachings and actions. Wright argues that Jesus's implicit and explicit kingdom narratives carried as part of their storyline the sense that his hearers were invited to see themselves as the "Israel" who would benefit from his work; and as the "helpers" who would have an active share in that work. It involved an invitation: the kingdom announcement which included the call to "repent and believe the good news." For those invited, there was also a welcome: Jesus's kingdom stories made it clear that everyone was a potential beneficiary, with the most striking examples being the poor and the sinners. Invitation and welcome gave birth to challenge: those who heard and accepted

---

178. Wright, *Jesus and the Victory of God*, loc. 11224.
179. Keener, *Acts: Exegetical Commentary*, 1:682.
180. Wright, *Jesus and the Victory of God*, loc. 9033.

were summoned to live as the renewed people of Israel. Finally, there was a summons generated. Some were called to go to Jerusalem to be his companions as his mission reached its climax. The crucial thing, of course, is that for Jesus, repentance, whether personal or national, did not involve going to the temple and offering sacrifice. Beginning with John's baptism, one could repent down by the Jordan instead of up in Jerusalem.[181] Zacchaeus was also restored on the spot.

E. P. Sanders argues that for Judaism, the kingdom was always the kingdom of Israel.[182] Jesus, by emphasizing the kingdom of God, made a fundamental change, one which broke with Jewish nationalism. This is significant considering the new Jerusalem/temple dwelling of the Holy Spirit in the eschatological age.

The coming of the kingdom of God is related to the Holy Spirit. It is through the Spirit that demons were cast out (Luke 11:20; Matt 12:28). Jesus spoke of the kingdom as imminent. When Jesus sent out the seventy-two, their message was, "The kingdom of God has come near to you" (Luke 10:9). In the Lord's prayer, they were to pray, "Thy kingdom come . . ." (Luke 11:2). In Acts, when Jesus spoke of the coming of the Holy Spirit, the question of the kingdom came up. Isaiah, Ezekiel, and Joel expected an outpouring of the Spirit associated with Israel's eschatological restoration. It is not difficult to understand why, when promised the Spirit, the disciples expected the coming of the kingdom.[183] Spirit anointing is for the proclamation of the kingdom to all peoples.

Christianized Version of the Jewish Spirit of Prophecy

Turner refers to E. Schweizer's teaching in *TDNT* that the Spirit of prophecy of the Old Testament that Luke emphasizes includes the Spirit only as empowering authoritative preaching.[184] He also

---

181. Wright, *Jesus and the Victory of God*, loc. 5428.
182. Sanders, *Jesus and Judaism*, 41.
183. Keener, "Prayer for the Spirit in Luke," loc. 3813.
184. Turner, "Spirit of Prophecy," 67, quoting Schweizer, "πνεῦμα," 408.

quotes Menzies's thesis that claims that in intertestamental Judaism the Spirit was known as the "Spirit of Prophecy" and that this led to the tendency to dissociate the Spirit from miracles and other works of power. Turner argues that the Spirit on the disciples is a version of the "Spirit of Prophecy." "It is also beyond dispute that any version of the Spirit of Prophecy available to Luke must ultimately come from Judaism."[185]

Turner rejects the idea that the Spirit of prophecy described by Luke was exclusively the power of inspired speech. He states that, traditionally, Luke 4:18–21 and Acts 10:38 were understood to imply that the Spirit was the power by which Jesus worked his redemptive miracles. He surveys Jewish literature and concludes,

> It would appear from this all-too-brief survey, that for a Jew to hold that the Spirit was received as the Spirit of Prophecy did not preclude him from attributing miracles to the same Spirit. For the Jew, the two conceptions do not appear to have seemed as foreign to each other as they may look to us.[186]

The argument that the Spirit in Acts was only prophetic and that all healings and miracles were done by the power ($\delta \acute{u} \nu \alpha \mu \iota \varsigma$) is unsubstantiated.[187] This argument is a result of asserting that Luke adopts the Jewish idea that the Spirit is the Spirit of prophecy[188] or the power of inspired insight or speech (glossolalia, prophecy, authoritative preaching).[189]

For Turner, the Spirit is not merely an empowering for mission, but also a charismatic presence that is necessary for the salvation/restoration of Israel.[190] Luke portrays the Spirit of prophecy as the charismatic power of Israel's restoration under her Davidic

---

185. Turner, "Spirit of Prophecy," 67.
186. Turner, "Spirit and the Power," 124.
187. Turner, "Spirit and the Power," 124–52.
188. Schweizer, "$\pi\nu\varepsilon\tilde{u}\mu\alpha$," 407.
189. Turner lists Schweizer, Haya-Prats, and R. P. Menzies as holding this view. Turner, "Spirit and the Power," 124–52.
190. Turner, *Power from on High*, 75.

Messiah/Mosaic prophet to legitimatize the church.[191] Turner represents theologians who believe in the baptism with the Holy Spirit as including salvation, gifts, and power. He does not support the distinct and separate view of the baptism with the Holy Spirit as classical Pentecostalism does.

Fee states that the Jewish people had a twofold understanding of the Spirit in the last days: (1) that the fullness of the Spirit would be upon the Messiah as the bearer of the Spirit (Isa 11:1–2; 42:1; 61:1–3); and (2) that part of the new covenant would be the outpouring of the Spirit on all of God's people (Ezek 36:26–27; Joel 2:28–30 [3:1–5a, LXX]). Fee states that John coined the phrase "baptism in the Spirit" as a metaphor taken from his sphere of activity.[192] He did so to contrast his activity with that of the Messiah who would usher in the coming age. Silva explains how Luke presents Pentecost as the beginning of a new epoch of salvation history.[193] This motif is evident in the distinction that Luke draws between the epoch of Jesus, ended by his ascension, and Pentecost, the beginning of the epoch of the Spirit.

Subproblem Four: Meaning of Jerusalem and the Temple

Jerusalem is an important topic for Luke concerning Jesus's ministry. Jesus was headed to the city of Jerusalem to redeem the remnant, create the new Israel, and send the Spirit to fill the redeemed and send them to evangelize the nations. All his time outside Jerusalem was spent proclaiming this message through his teaching and by displaying signs and wonders to all Israel.

Ben Meyer states that the centrality of the temple to the life of Israel was due to its claim to the divine presence, hence its claim to be the source of holiness, its call to worship, and its pointing back to the beginning and forward to the end. Jesus had a deep

---

191. Turner, "'Spirit of Prophecy' as the Power," 328.
192. Fee, *Gospel and Spirit*, 112–13.
193. Silva, "πεντηκοστή," 712.

reverence for the temple and its cultus, which was evident in his participation in the temple feasts and indeed in his "cleansing" of the pavilion of the temple. On the other hand, there was Jesus's independence of the standard view of the temple priesthood and state. "An instance is his sovereign comportment respecting the forgiveness of sins in word and act" (Luke 7:36–42, 47–48; 9:9; 10:3).[194]

What was Jesus doing early on in his ministry and later after Jerusalem? Because of the meaning of Jerusalem, everything that Jesus did away from Jerusalem acquired new meaning.[195] Jesus proclaimed the Word of YHWH and allowed all of Israel to see the signs and wonders. The outpouring of the Spirit in the upper room[196] rather than at the temple was significant in and of itself. The place where the presence of God was to be found was in the temple. The temple was the place of worship, forgiveness, restoration, and dedication. In addition to all that was going on down by the River Jordan (John's baptism) and the healings and forgiveness offered by Jesus throughout Galilee and Samaria—now the Spirit was poured out in a powerful, visible, and public manner. The expected place for such an important event would be the temple. Especially for those who came from the diaspora in celebration of the Pentecost festival, this happening in the upper room and not the temple might be indicative that something new was happening. Peter's sermon explains that a new eschatological age had arrived—all based on Joel's proclamation (of the INE).

Luke shows Jesus headed to Jerusalem throughout his Gospel. In the light of the INE that is in Luke, Jesus was headed to Jerusalem to redeem the remnant, and everything that he does before Luke 9:51 prepares the way. Acts 2:22 says, "Men of Israel, listen to these words: Jesus the Nazarene, a man attested to you by God with

---

194. Meyer, "Temple," 230.

195. Wright, *New Testament and the People of God*, 210.

196. Longenecker, "Acts," 735, argues for the "upper room" as the place where the Spirit descended. He shows normal Lukan usage of ἱερόν to refer to the temple and οἶκος as the word used in Acts 2:2. See also Polhill, *Acts*, 97; Bock, *Acts*, 95; Pervo, *Acts*, 59.

miracles and wonders and signs which God performed through Him in your midst, just as you yourselves know." This verse comes right after the Joel quotation in Acts 2:17–21, "'. . . it shall be in the last days,' God says, 'that I will pour forth of My Spirit upon all mankind . . . and I will grant wonders in the sky above, and signs on the earth beneath.'" Luke links "miracles, signs, and wonders" with the outpouring of the Spirit. He also links Jesus's ministry with that which happened on the day of Pentecost.

Wright traces how Luke (as well as the other evangelists) wove the symbolic value of Jerusalem, Mount Zion, and the temple itself into his writings. He states, "The three aspects of the temple that have particular significance are the presence of YHWH, the sacrificial system, and the temple's political significance." First, the temple was regarded as the dwelling place of Israel's covenant God. The symbolic nature of the temple established the sacred precinct as being located at the "cosmic center of the universe, at the place where heaven and earth converge and thus form where God's control over the universe is effected."[197]

Second, the temple was a place of sacrifice. It was the place where forgiveness of sins on the one hand, and cleansing from defilement on the other, were believed to be effected. The temple was the center of the national hope, the governing eschatology, as well as of the national life and identity; and at the heart of the temple's existence and significance there stood the sacrificial system.[198]

Third, the temple possessed political significance. If the one true God dwells in a particular building, the people responsible for the building acquire great prestige. "It was bound up inextricably with the royal house, and with royal aspirations."[199] It is for this reason that Jesus's actions in relation to the temple must be treated with the utmost seriousness.

Wright notes that the themes that should be considered about Jesus's action in the temple are purity, money, sacrificial animals, symbolic destruction, coming kingdom. As a prophet, Jesus

197. Wright, *Jesus and the Victory of God*, loc. 8580.
198. Wright, *Jesus and the Victory of God*, loc. 8594.
199. Wright, *Jesus and the Victory of God*, loc. 8675.

acted out a parable of judgment on the temple. "When Jesus went to Jerusalem, he symbolically and prophetically enacted judgment upon it—a judgment which he announced verbally as well as in action."[200] Jesus was announcing with prophetic authority but also with kingdom authority. In Jesus's ministry, the Abrahamic, Mosaic, and Davidic themes merge.

Concerning judgment on the temple, Bockmuehl speaks of the corruption that was present.[201] Of key significance was the fact that of the twenty-eight high priests between 37 BC and AD 70, all but two came from the four power-hungry, illegitimate, non-Zadokite families. Recent historical study makes it clear that the operation of the temple, which most devout Jews regarded as the physical center of their religious practice, was in the hands of a vast economic and religious power network. The legitimate and necessary operation of the temple was supported by a maze of intrigue, nepotism, and corruption, which is amply reflected in Josephus, Qumran documents, and early rabbinic sources.[202]

Jesus affirms temple worship as divinely appointed and yet claims superiority over the temple. Portrayed in Luke 19:47, Luke explicitly presents Jesus's teaching in the temple καθ' ἡμέραν, or "daily." Luke presents a cleansing and reclaiming of the temple. Even though the apostles frequent the temple in Acts, Stephen argues that the Most High does not dwell in houses (e.g., Isa 66:1–2) and insists that the temple is only temporary.

Jesus is heading toward Jerusalem to unite Israel but also to judge between the remnant and the idolatrous leaders in Israel. Early on in his ministry, Jesus speaks of a restored Israel. He teaches and performs signs and wonders in the presence of the people before and after his death on the cross. The nation has time to hear what Jesus was doing and what was to happen in Jerusalem. After the death, resurrection, and ascension of Jesus, the process was finished and confirmed with the descent of the Holy Spirit on the day of Pentecost.

200. Wright, *Jesus and the Victory of God*, loc. 8783.
201. Bockmuehl, *This Jesus*, 69.
202. Bockmuehl, *This Jesus*, 70.

Jerusalem as a place of God's presence is no longer. Israel and the temple are now the church. The coming of the Spirit on the day of Pentecost was the new creation of Israel and the new Jerusalem. Since Jesus had pronounced judgment on the temple, something new was in mind. Jesus would build the new temple; his people would be the new Jerusalem. This is the promised restoration of Israel. It is not a replacement, but rather a restoration through Jesus—the remnant.

This study focuses on God's plan to transfer blessing from Israel to a universal group that includes Israel and the gentiles. It was God's plan from the beginning that Israel's role as the people of God would be restored through the Messiah to be a blessing to the nations—this according to the promise to Abraham. Identifying the INE as argument for Luke-Acts argues for an economic rather than punitive supracessionism.[203] Judgment is for those who reject Jesus after having the teaching and signs presented to them. This study does not agree that there is no plan for national Israel. It is clear that God so loved the world and Israel is a key topic in the history of the world. It has always been important to YHWH to preserve the nation of Israel as a testimony to world (e.g., Exod 32:11).

Markus Bockmuehl argues that the Essene community already had a concept of a "living temple," but there is no evidence that they influenced the early Christian movement.[204] Timothy Wardle studies the "pattern of dissent from the Jerusalem temple resulting in the construction of alternate temples."[205] In the Second Temple period, there were other temples: Elephantine, the Samaritan temple, and the temple at Leontopolis. He studies the Qumran period as well. He attempts to show that the construction of the early Christian sense of itself as a temple was along the same lines. He argues that "the formation of alternative temples outside of Jerusalem follows a common pattern, as similar motivations

---

203. Vlach, "Various Forms of Replacement Theology," 57–69.
204. Bockmuehl, *This Jesus*, 115.
205. Wardle, *Jerusalem Temple*, 4.

contributed to each community's separation from Jerusalem and establishment of a new temple."[206]

Wardle's thesis is "that as the formation of alternative temples was the result of specific instances of conflict with the Jerusalem religious establishment, then it stands to reason that the early Christian temple ideology was borne of similar convictions."[207] He argues that the Christian use of temple terminology should be understood as a continuation of Jesus's critique of the chief priests of his time and also as a reaction to their part in the crucifixion of Jesus and their ongoing hostility toward the early church in Jerusalem.

Wright seeks to find a reason for the replacement of the temple that is more in line with the plan of God throughout Scripture:

1. Jesus intended to symbolize the imminent destruction of the temple.
2. He believed that Israel's God was in the process of judging and redeeming his people, not just as one such incident among many, but as the climax of Israel's whole history.
3. The judgment on the temple would take the form of destruction by Rome, which (like Babylon, according to Jeremiah) would be the agent of the wrath of YHWH.
4. The specific reasons for this judgment were, broadly, Israel's failure to obey YHWH's call to be his people; more narrowly, Israel's large-scale commitment to national rebellion, coupled with her failure to enact justice within her society, not least within the temple system itself.
5. Jesus symbolized the destruction of the temple as a part of the INE's eschatological program.[208]

E. P. Sanders proposes that the best explanation of Jesus's demonstrative action in the temple and his saying against the temple is regarding eschatological expectation.[209] The kingdom was at

---

206. Wardle, *Jerusalem Temple*, 10.
207. Wardle, *Jerusalem Temple*, 10.
208. Wright, *Jesus and the Victory of God*, loc. 8793.
209. Sanders, *Jesus and Judaism*, 77.

hand and, among other things, it meant that the old temple would be replaced by a new one.

Silva accents the importance of Jerusalem. He says, "Jesus had to go to Jerusalem to fulfill his mission there at the center of the world of OT Jewish faith (Luke 9:31). There he confronted the two theocratic institutions: the priests as functionaries of the cult (e.g., Luke 19:45), and the scribes as keepers of the Mosaic tradition. His sacrifice only made sense and was effective in Jerusalem."[210]

In Jerusalem, through the cross, the cult of the temple and the law are judged by God. Jerusalem is especially important to the theology of Luke—at the beginning (1:5–25) and the end (24:53) he refers to the city.

Wright claims, "The temple has been rebuilt; the Messiah has come at last."[211] He posits this as the theme of Luke. It is a common theme in the NT. His welcome to join the remnant was a sign that forgiveness, restoration, and return from exile were all happening. The time of the new covenant had arrived. In the new eschatological age, Jesus was bypassing the temple by forgiving and restoring lives without animal sacrifices. According to Wright, Jesus's celebratory meals are the equivalent, in real life, of the homecoming party in the parable of the prodigal son.

Jerusalem is central to the new exodus. Silva[212] records the use of "Jerusalem" in the NT. The noun "form Ἰερουσαλήμ is used c. 77x and 64 of the occurrences are found in Luke-Acts . . . . The hellenized form Ἱεροσόλυμα occurs c. 62x mainly in Acts . . . . The choice of one form over the other cannot be determined."

Jerusalem was the center of Jewish faith (Matt 16:21; Luke 9:31). Silva states, "Jesus had to go to Jerusalem for his sacrifice made sense and was effective only in Jerusalem (Mark 10:33–34), yet this sacrifice was rejected by the leaders in the city while accepted by God, as the accounts of the resurrection testify (e.g., also Mark 8:31)."[213]

---

210. Silva, "Ἰερουσαλήμ," 524.
211. Wright, *Jesus and the Victory of God*, loc. 2846.
212. Silva, "Ἰερουσαλήμ," 524, cf. BDAG s.v. Ἱεροσόλυμα.
213. Silva, "Ἰερουσαλήμ," 524.

Jerusalem is the setting in which the corrupt power brokers of Judaism are confronted in Jesus's ministry (Luke 11:15-18) and are judged by God himself in the crucifixion. Jerusalem is especially important in the theology of Luke, whose Gospel begins and ends with reference to events that took place in the temple (Luke 1:5-25; 24:53), and there are numerous significant allusions to the city throughout the book (e.g., 2:22, 38; 9:31, 51; 13:33-34; 18:31; 23:38; 24:47). Luke's point seems clear: "The promise given to the ancient people of God is fulfilled in the history of Jesus and His church."[214]

Lohse states, "The true Israel assembles in the holy place." Acts goes further in this direction, for here Jerusalem serves as the place that "links the history of Jesus with the beginning of that of the community."[215] Hence, Jesus's disciples, to whom he had appeared after his resurrection, remained at his express command in Jerusalem (Luke 24:49, 52) to wait for the outpouring of the Holy Spirit (Acts 1:4; 2:1-4). In accordance with their commission, they proclaimed the divine events to all peoples beginning from Jerusalem (Luke 24:47; Acts 5:20-21). In Heb 13:14, we read that believers "are looking for the city that is to come." At the same time, the community has already come to Zion, the heavenly Jerusalem. The new Jerusalem is the city in which the new covenant has been made through the blood of Jesus.[216]

This study seeks the meaning of Jerusalem for Luke. The importance of Jerusalem to Luke-Acts has not been explained in relation to the baptism with the Holy Spirit. In Luke, there is an emphasis on Jerusalem. This is a major issue for Luke. Perhaps where classical Pentecostals have fallen short has been the failure to explain the major emphasis in Luke: Why Jesus must go to Jerusalem. The most probable proposed design by this study is that Luke intends to show that the death, resurrection, enthronement, and coming of the Spirit—all from Jerusalem—denote the arrival of the INE.

214. Silva, "Ἰερουσαλήμ," 525.
215. Lohse, "Σιών," 331.
216. Lohse, "Σιών," 334.

Jerusalem is the place for the restoration of Israel. In the city, he will unite Israel and judge between the remnant and the idolatrous leaders. Early in his ministry, Jesus brings salvation to all Israel and gives time for the whole nation to hear YHWH and to see and experience his signs and wonders. The nation has time to hear what YHWH is doing and will complete in Jerusalem (INE). This is significant to the meaning of Jesus's baptism with the Holy Spirit and fire.

Jerusalem in Isaiah and Luke becomes the unifying goal of the new exodus: the enthronement of the king; the shift and transformation of the kingdom, of the nation (judgment of Israel), of the city, of the temple, of YHWH's atonement for sin (the death and resurrection); where the exaltation to the throne (ascension), the coming of the Spirit, and empowerment of the believers and commission to evangelize Jewish people and the gentiles occur. From beginning to end, all happens in Jerusalem/Zion—no division of Spirit activity. Jerusalem joins Spirit baptism for regeneration and empowerment for service. Everything happens in Jerusalem. The goal of Jesus's ministry of gathering the remnant, restoring Israel, and redeeming humankind is the sending of the Spirit that impels the church to be a blessing to the nations of the world.

Summary

The new exodus complete with the filling of the Spirit is the promised redemption, restoration, and empowerment for mission. It is the new covenant promise to the remnant of Israel and includes the salvation for Jerusalem, the restoration of Israel, and the inclusion of the gentiles within the people of God. This is what is promised in Acts 1:8 and is the outline—hermeneutical grid—for the book of Acts following the new exodus of Isaiah.

The fulfillment of the promised plan of God is a major theme of Luke-Acts. This is part of the declaration of purpose that Luke provides in Luke-Acts. The Septuagint style of Luke suggests the continuity between the ongoing work of God and the Old

Testament Scriptures. This is related directly to the argument of Luke-Acts.

A most probable design for Luke is the INE as a paradigm pattern for Luke-Acts. Isaiah 40 serves as a hermeneutical lens without which the entire Lukan program cannot be properly understood. The Isaianic program is the hermeneutical framework in which isolated events are interpreted. In Luke 4:16–30, Luke introduces the framework in which his writings should be understood. All five clauses in this Isaianic quotation refer to the arrival of the salvation of God.[217] This allows Luke to emphasize the new era as a legitimate continuation of the history of the people of God.

Stargel traces the new exodus themes throughout the Old Testament Scriptures showing that the new exodus was remembered by command (Exod 12:14–20) and as an identity story.[218] The identity song in Exod 15:1–21 invites ongoing participation in the exodus. Even those who had never been in Egypt saw themselves as having been liberated from there.

When described in Acts 1:5, 8, this baptism with the Holy Spirit caused the disciples to ask about the "restoration of the kingdom to Israel." There was a definite eschatological new covenant fulfillment related to the baptism with the Holy Spirit. It brought redemption and cleansing to Israel's remnant and the fulfillment of the INE narrative.

The Jewish people understood that the Messiah would be the bearer of the Spirit (Isa 11:1–2; 42:1; 61:1–3). The new covenant would be known by the outpouring of the Spirit (Ezek 36:26–27; Joel 2:28–30 [3:1–5a, LXX]). The metaphor of baptism with the Spirit and fire describes the arrival of YHWH—the Messiah and Davidic King. Fee states that John coined the phrase "baptized in the Spirit" as a metaphor to compare his activity with that of the Messiah who would usher in the coming age.[219]

The baptism with the Holy Spirit is a part of the salvation (new exodus) experience promised to the remnant of Israel. This

---

217. Pao, *Acts and the Isaianic New Exodus*, 71.
218. Stargel, "Construction of Exodus Identity," 174.
219. Fee, *Gospel and Spirit*, 113.

study proposes that it is the crown of the new exodus experience and at the same time it describes the INE as a whole. It is necessary for mission and should be received at once after accepting Jesus as a personal savior. As such, the "filling of the Spirit" is a part of the WOL/INE, and it is subsequent in order to the initial conversion experience.

The new exodus is another way of saying new creation or new covenant. It is part of Jewish salvation history that is being carried to consummation. Entrance is through the Spirit in conviction, repentance, regeneration, and infilling, which brings enduement of power and the centrifugal mission of Israel to the nations—all united theologically by the INE theme.

Chapter 3

Exegesis of Luke

Introduction

IS THE BAPTISM WITH the Spirit united with regeneration as a part of a multidimensional salvation and empowerment process? Luke connects Simeon's prophecy with Acts 2 as the fulfillment of the INE. The new covenant included the gathering of the remnant and reformation (new creation) of Israel, redemption on the cross, and light to the gentiles—all through the Spirit. This chapter follows Luke's argument in the light of INE themes and interprets the baptism with the Holy Spirit on the day of Pentecost in relation to the new covenant or INE.

No Pentecostal has emphasized Jerusalem to the meaning of baptism with the Spirit. Luke has Jerusalem in view throughout his Gospel. Early in his ministry, Jesus offers salvation to all Israel and allows the whole nation to hear YHWH and see and experience his signs, wonders, and teaching. He seeks the remnant of Israel to include them on the "way" or INE. His work reaches its peak in Jerusalem (both in the crucifixion and at Pentecost). The gospel goes out first to the Jews, and through the restored remnant, blessings flow to the rest of the earth. The outpouring on the day of Pentecost occurs in Jerusalem, outside of the temple, and to a Jewish remnant. The coming of the Spirit on the day of Pentecost confirmed the reign of Jesus as Davidic Messiah and Lord—the new eschatological age had arrived, and Isaiah's prophecy was being fulfilled. Prophetic messages of judgment are spoken and acted out by Jesus. In Jerusalem, the remnant was filled with the Spirit, the wicked Jewish leaders were judged, and the kingdom became the new Israel ready to evangelize the gentiles. God's promises in Isaiah were fulfilled. The spiritual (new) Jerusalem appeared. Jerusalem as the center of the plan will be key to the interpretation of this exegetical section. In Jerusalem, Jesus does two things: he ushers in the new exodus and empowers the remnant for mission, and he judges all who reject YHWH, including idolatrous Israel. Jerusalem provides unity from beginning to end—all through the pouring out of the Spirit.

This chapter begins with the subject of the arrival of the consolation of Israel and a comparison between Jesus's and John's baptisms. Then it surveys Jesus's ministry to identify a progression of actions and teaching in line with the INE. Jesus's ministry can be divided into three parts. (1) The first part is the gathering of the remnant outside of Jerusalem (the agrarian population—towns, and villages, mainly in Galilee). He travels and offers salvation (entrance to the new exodus) via word and deed. He performs healings and exorcisms, forgives sins, and shares celebration meals. (2) The second part is in the city of Jerusalem beginning with the transfiguration, triumphal entry, cleansing of the temple, and finally, his crucifixion. (3) The third part is the post-resurrection encounter with his disciples and the anticipation of the promise of the Father, the ascension and sending the Spirit.

The Consolation of Israel

The arrival of the "consolation of Israel" introduces the INE theme both in Isaiah and in Luke. Simeon declares that the "consolation of Israel had arrived" (Luke 2:25, 29–32) citing from Isa 40:1, "'Comfort, O comfort My people,' says your God." From this initial quote, what follows in Luke-Acts unfolds the plan of the ages eschatologized by Isaiah in the INE. The parallels between the INE and Luke-Acts argue for Luke's intention to show the coming of the new eschatological era. Jesus's baptism with the Holy Spirit and fire is placed in the context of the INE, which involves judgment (fire) and transformation for salvation and empowerment (Spirit). The significance of the baptism with the Holy Spirit in Luke is best understood in relation to the context, which is the new covenant as described by Isaiah (INE).

Jesus was the greater one to come. He was the consolation of Israel mentioned at the beginning of Luke. Following the first quote, there is another reference from Isaiah's introduction to the INE that is included in Luke. When Luke quoted Isa 40:3–5, it placed John the Baptist's and Jesus's ministries in that context,

> The voice of one calling in the wilderness
> Make ready the way of the Lord
> Make his paths straight
> Every ravine shall be filled up,
> And every mountain and hill shall be brought low;
> And the crooked shall become straight,
> And the rough roads smooth;
> And all flesh shall see the salvation of God.

This passage places John the Baptist within the INE. The LXX translated "Lord" for the Hebrew YHWH.[1] The theme of John's preaching was repentance, judgment, and the coming of the greater one.

The purpose of John's baptism was to reveal Jesus to Israel. He was prophetically enacting the coming exodus that YHWH would bring for his people. Repentance brought salvation from the wrath to come through the power of the Spirit. Jesus's baptism in water was a pattern. John's baptism was not for gentile proselytes; rather, it was for Jews who were repenting. It was a rite that involved becoming part of a community awaiting the promised Messiah.

---

1. For discussion on Jesus as Jehovah see Strong, *Systematic Theology*, 309.

John the Baptist and Jesus Compared

Luke chapter 3 compares John's baptism with Jesus's through μεν/ δε. The comparison is made between (1) the baptizers: the forerunner and Jesus (the one more powerful—YHWH—the second person of the Trinity incarnate); (2) the means: in water (type) and with Spirit (antitype); (3) the purpose: preparation and the fulfillment that is salvation and judgment.

Luke states that the axe is already at the root of the trees (Luke 3:9) when speaking of how God can raise children for Abraham "out of these stones." The imminent judgment could be avoided only on an individual basis by repenting in the name of Jesus (e.g., Acts 19:4). For Luke, the baptism with the Holy Spirit and fire was thus best understood as involving two separate groups within Israel. For the "wheat" there is the blessing of the Spirit, whereas for the "chaff" there is the judgment of burning. Jesus had come to bring a new eschatological age that included judgment upon national Israel and the temple and salvation and fulfillment of the prophecy of Isaiah.

Both Matthew and Luke arrange their material with the judgment motif before and after the comparison of the baptisms. These make an *inclusio* of material significant to the theme. The judgment that is described in the parables of Luke (13:6–30; 19:12–27; 20:9–18) implies a shift of the identity of the people of God and the temple from its former (earthly) state to a spiritual one. In Luke 23:45, the veil of the temple was torn in two. The place where the presence of God had been was no more. Never again would temple sacrifices, worship, and restoration of sinners be effectual. It was a new eschatological era.

The judgment metaphor appears in Luke 13:28–30:

> There will be weeping and gnashing of teeth there when you see Abraham and Isaac and Jacob and all the prophets in the kingdom of God, and yourselves being cast out. And they will come from east and west, and from north and south, and will recline at table in the kingdom of God. And behold, some are last who will be first and some are first who will be last.

This addresses what Spirit and fire means and what it applies to. This brief parable/extended metaphor tells us the meaning. The meaning of Spirit baptism is related to the way of the Lord/ INE or salvation for Israel and the nations. The meaning of fire is judgment.

There is more emphasis on judgment in Luke 3 than on salvation. John rejected the Pharisees who were coming without repentance. He would not baptize them in water without fruit worthy of repentance and warned them that true judgment for incredulous Israel was coming. He was only a forerunner, but Jesus would bring in the new age and only the believing remnant would be saved. The reward of repentance was the Spirit which the water represented. The salvation of Israel through the INE involved judgment on national Israel. Jesus fulfilled everything the temple and its sacrificial system represented. To reject Jesus was to stay behind without the presence of God in the temple, the city, or the nation.

The constant emphasis throughout Jesus's ministry was that those who follow him would escape judgment. The time of the Spirit was coming. Isaiah 4:4 combines washing, cleansing, judgment, and fire. The comparison between the water and the Spirit emerges again in Isa 44:3, "For I will pour water on the thirsty land and streams on the dry ground; I will pour out My Spirit on your offspring, and My blessing on your descendants."

The INE is not one of fire and Spirit; rather it is the rejection of Jesus that brings fire. Malachi 3:2-3; 4:1 (3:19 LXX) includes both refining and destructive action on two groups of people:

> But who can endure the day of His coming? And who can stand when He appears? For He is like a refiner's fire and like fuller's soap. And here we sit as a smelter and purifier of silver, and He will purify the sons of Levi and refine them like gold and silver so that they may present to the Lord offerings in righteousness. "For behold the day is coming, burning like a furnace and all the arrogant and every evildoer will be chaff; and the day that is coming will set them ablaze," says the Lord of hosts, "so that it will leave them neither root nor branch."

Both salvation and judgment are symbolized by these images. Fire represents judgment (the cutting and burning of trees—root, branch, and of the chaff) and Spirit is for comfort. The consolation of Israel involves purification through Jesus's death and the coming of the Spirit—a new creation in Isaiah. Among those who receive judgment are those who reject Jesus as Lord, both now and at the end of the age.

Luke 3:16 states, "ἀπεκρίνατο λέγων πᾶσιν ὁ Ἰωάννης, Ἐγὼ μὲν ὕδατι βαπτίζω ὑμᾶς ... αὐτὸς ὑμᾶς βαπτίσει ἐν πνεύματι ἁγίῳ καὶ πυρί.'" The preposition ἐν has significance.[2] For Daniel Wallace, Christ is the agent (since αὐτός is the subject), and the Holy Spirit is the means that the Lord uses to baptize.[3] This study argues for the use of the dative of means with the preposition ἐν in Luke in agreement with Wallace. The dative of means is best translated "with" indicating how something was done. This supports the entire new exodus—the Spirit becomes the center of the whole event including salvation and mission to the world. Wallace also quotes 1 Cor 12:13 γὰρ ἐν ἑνὶ πνεύματι ἡμεῖς πάντες εἰς ἓν σῶμα ἐβαπτίσθημεν ("for by one Spirit we were baptized into one body"). He contends that this is an illustration of ἐν used for means.[4] The Holy Spirit is the means that Jesus Christ uses to baptize. First Corinthians 12:13 is the fulfillment of Mark 1:8. "For we were all baptized by one Spirit into one body—whether Jews or Greeks, slave or free—and we were all given the one Spirit to drink."

It is the age of the Spirit. That is the characteristic of the INE/new covenant. This is in line with the new creation promised by

---

2. All of the Gospels have the preposition with Jesus's baptism; only two (Matthew and John) have the preposition with both baptisms—John's and Jesus's. Matthew has Holy Spirit and fire describing Jesus's baptism and hostile Pharisees and Sadducees in the group. Mark does not mention fire or the axe and winnowing fork and neither the Pharisees or Sadducees among the crowd. Luke has the hostile group, and he adds the axe at the root of the trees and winnowing fork and unquenchable fire together with the baptism of Holy Spirit and fire. John includes a group of priests and Levites that had been sent by the Pharisees; however, he does not mention judgment until chapter 3.

3. Wallace, *Greek Grammar Beyond the Basics*, 373.

4. Wallace, *Greek Grammar Beyond the Basics*, 373.

Isaiah. In the creation of the world, the second person of the Trinity (later hypostatically united to humanity and incarnate as Jesus) was the agent, and the Holy Spirit was the means. John makes it clear that everything was created through Jesus as agent (John 1). Genesis speaks of how the Spirit hovered over the face of the waters. In the new creation, in like manner, Jesus is the baptizer, and the Spirit is the means. The main characteristic of the INE is the Spirit (Isa 32:15; 44:3; Ezek 18:31; 36:25–27; 37:14; 39:29; Joel 2:28).

In Luke 7:18–35, when the disciples of John went to Jesus to ask if he was the one to come, Jesus responded, "Go and report to John what you have seen and heard: the blind receive sight, the lame walk, the lepers are cleansed, and the deaf hear, the dead are raised up, and the poor have the gospel preached to them. 'And blessed is he who keeps from stumbling over Me.'" Pao[5] argues that this list should be understood as the manifestation of the arrival of salvation for Israel. Jesus's response alludes to Isa 61:1, where the arrival of the new era is characterized by the words and deeds that were characteristic of his ministry. The forgiveness and salvation of the sinful woman in front of the Pharisee was an announcement as to the coming of the new exodus and was an opportunity for salvation for the Pharisee. Jesus was offering salvation and restoration outside the temple. The temple system was being replaced by one in this new eschatological era.

Gathering the Remnant

Jesus spent much time in the villages and towns of Galilee preaching and confirming with signs and wonders that the INE had arrived. He was gathering the remnant for the restoration of Israel and light for the nations. Even though the power brokers of Jerusalem had almost no presence in Galilee, Jesus was still rejected by the Jews. When rejected at Nazareth he explained that no prophet was accepted in his hometown. Then he went on to show that

---

5. Pao, *Acts and the Isaianic New Exodus*, 74.

Elijah and Elisha both ministered to gentiles. The gentiles were predestined to be a part of the people of God—this beginning in Scripture with God's promise to Abraham.

Luke emphasizes the universal nature of God's salvific purpose. It is important to note that the restoration of Israel begins with the remnant—Jesus. The parallels between Jesus and Israel in the desert temptation are significant. Where Israel failed the test, Jesus did not. Where Jesus obeyed and followed the Spirit's guidance, Israel "rebelled and grieved his Holy Spirit" (Isa 63:10). Green lists similarities of the testing of Israel in the desert and Jesus. (1) Israel experienced hunger to learn that one does not live by bread alone (Deut 8:3); (2) Israel was instructed to worship the one and only God (Deut 6:4–15); and (3) Israel was commanded not to put the Lord God to the test (Deut 6:6).[6] In each case, Israel failed (e.g., Exod 17:1–7; Deut 9:6–29; e.g., Acts 7:35, 39–43). Jesus the true Son of God fulfilled the destiny of Israel. Jesus was the remnant of Israel tested in preparation for the restored people of God, and he did not fail.

The temptation narrative depicts a victorious Jesus turning back the forces of darkness, preparing the way for the liberation of his people. From then forward, he gathers God's people. This claim is evidenced in Luke 5:1–11, where the calling of the disciples is a means of satisfying the primary objective (e.g., Luke 9:1–6). Jesus calls Peter to be a "catcher of men."

The Inauguration in the Synagogue

Luke 4:13–30 begins Jesus's ministry with the theme of rejection of the prophet by the people of God. In Jesus's address (Luke 4:24–27), the role of Elijah and Elisha as agents of healing to outsiders is important. Elijah is sent to a woman, a non-Jew, a widow—surely a person of low status. Elisha also ministers to a non-Jew—a Syrian with leprosy (which distanced him even further). Jesus uses these

---

6. Green, *Gospel of Luke*, 193.

examples to emphasize that "good news to the poor" embraces the widow, the unclean, the gentile, and those of the lowest status.

Lukan scholars recognize the importance of this passage in the structure of Luke-Acts.[7] Stronstad states that "Jesus identifies himself as a prophet in his inaugural sermon at Nazareth" (Luke 4:16ff).[8] This expands the healing, exorcism, or teaching to include a symbolic and prophetic meaning as well as fulfilling real, felt temporal needs. Acts 3:22-23 identifies Jesus as the prophet like Moses (e.g., Acts 7:37).

Jesus was born of the Spirit, filled with the Spirit (at his baptism), and led by the Spirit into the wilderness to be tempted by the devil. When he had resisted the devil victoriously, he returned to Galilee, "in the power of the Spirit" (Luke 4:14). Jesus taught, healed, and lived by the power of the Spirit.

He went to Nazareth and entered the synagogue where he stood up to read. The book of Isaiah was handed to him and he opened the book and found where it is written,

> The Spirit of the Lord is upon Me because He anointed Me to preach the gospel to the poor. He has sent Me to proclaim release to the captives, and recovery of sight to the blind. To set free those who are downtrodden, to proclaim the favorable year of the Lord. (Isa 61:1-2)

Joel Green notes that the repeated reference to "release" (ἄφεσις) (e.g., Luke 4:18) has significance to the plan of salvation.[9] Release is often translated as "forgiveness" in the rest of Luke-Acts (Luke 1:77; 3:3; 24:47; Acts 2:38; 5:31; 10:43; 13:38; 26:18). Jesus is the Savior who grants forgiveness of sins. It also is set in opposition to the binding power of Satan (Luke 13:10-17; Acts 10:38). A main theological feature of Jesus's work is the "release from debts." This includes the freeing of slaves, the cancellation of debts, and the returning of the land to its original owners. The jubilee theme is most evident in 4:8-19 by the repeated use of "release" and by

---

7. Pao, *Acts and the Isaianic New Exodus*, 71.
8. Stronstad, *Prophethood of All Believers*, 13.
9. Green, *Gospel of Luke*, 212.

"the year of the Lord's favor" (Isa 61:2). "It is now widely recognized that Isaiah 58 and 61 develop jubilee themes, describing the coming redemption from exile and captivity in eschatological language."[10] The long-awaited epoch of salvation had been inaugurated. It began with Jesus's birth.

Luke 4:14–28 is significant as a pattern for the ministry of Jesus and the early church. Liefeld and Pao argue that in Luke 4:13–30 there is a paradigm for the rest of Luke-Acts: (1) the presentation of the gospel to Jews in their synagogues, (2) rejection, and (3) turning to the wider gentile world (e.g., Acts 13:46).[11] This event is not limited to the ministry of Jesus; it also serves as a theological introduction to the early Christian movement as recorded in Acts.

Jesus Offers the Promised Salvation in Towns and Villages

At the beginning of his ministry (Luke 4:31–43), Jesus displayed salvation to all Israel beginning with the towns and villages. Through the power of the Spirit, he cast out demons and healed many. The ultimate destination was Jerusalem to finish the work, but he had to show all Israel and Judah God's promised salvation. His works were such that when he tried to leave Capernaum, they tried to prevent him. He said to them, "I must preach the kingdom of God to the other cities also, for I was sent for this purpose." Jesus was gathering the remnant to be saved.

Even though there was some opposition to Jesus in the towns and villages, the patrons in the patronage system (the power brokers and temple leaders) were in Jerusalem and the most receptive to the message in the agrarian areas. Jerusalem had kingdom significance, but the disciples were from Galilee. Jesus was gathering the remnant, and it was important to gather the remnant who would become the new people of God and evangelize the world.

---

10. Green, *Gospel of Luke*, 212.
11. Liefeld and Pao, "Luke," 121.

Signs and Wonders

The Cleansing of a Leper. In Luke 5:12–16, Jesus touches the leper to heal him. Since there is no precedent of this except perhaps in John's ministry (he is the first to "baptize"—people always baptized themselves), Jesus displays mediator (παράκλησις) characteristics. Jesus touches as he heals and later his disciples do the same through the Spirit upon them. It is an announcement to all that the kingdom has come through signs and wonders and that Jesus is the Messiah (Isa 61:1–3).

The healing of the leper fits the description of Isaiah, "good news to the afflicted; liberty to captives; and freedom to prisoners." Significantly, Jesus encounters the leper on the outside of the city (most likely). This was far from the temple. By doing so, he was already announcing the new exodus and providing an opportunity to enter in through faith. Jesus heals and pronounces the man clean. Then he tells him to go to the priests and make an offering as Moses commanded, "for a testimony to them."

Power to Heal and Authority to Forgive. Jesus's power to heal and authority to forgive sins are significant Isaianic signs of eschatological salvation (e.g., Isa 42:1–4; Matt 12:15–18, 28, 31–32; Luke 4:18; 7:22; 1 Cor 12:9–10, 28). In Luke 5:17–26, teachers of the law were present from all Judea, Galilee, and Jerusalem. In the healing of the paralytic, Jesus also forgives sin. Then Jesus said, "Which is easier to say, 'Your sins have been forgiven you,' or to say, 'Rise up and walk?'" The Pharisees and the teachers of the law said that Jesus was blasphemous for only God can forgive sin. This was a proclamation of the kingdom having come and the new exodus underway. In Luke 5:17, the phrase "power of the Lord" is synonymous with "Spirit of the Lord." This is clear from Lukan usage elsewhere (e.g., 1:17, 35; 4:14; 24:49; Acts 1:8; 10:38).[12] He offers salvation to representatives of all Israel/Judah. Their rejection of him is also indicative of the inevitable baptism

---

12. Green, *Gospel of Luke*, 240.

with fire (judgment) coming upon Jerusalem. Luke juxtaposes the calling of Jesus's disciples and opposition.

Luke adds an INE theme in Luke 5 that Matthew and Mark do not mention. Luke mentions that as the formerly paralyzed man walks home, he was praising God. Luke records the gratitude and joy that come with the saving action of God (e.g., Luke 2:20; 4:15; 5:26; 7:16; 13:13; 17:15; 18:43; 23:47; Acts 4:21; 11:15–18; 21:20). Joy is a characteristic mentioned above in the INE theme.

Inclusion of the Outcasts. In Luke chapter 7 in the healing of the centurion's servant, Jesus was disregarding all limits formerly set concerning accepting hospitality in a gentile's home. Jesus failed to draw insider-outsider lines, even when faced with possible gentile defilement as well as potential corpse impurity in the healing of the widow's son.[13] In the miracle of the centurion, there is an almost exact parallel with the healing of Naaman in Elisha's ministry. In the raising of the widow's son, "they were all filled with awe and praised God. 'A great prophet has appeared among us,' they said. 'God has come to help his people.' This news about Jesus spread throughout Judea and the surrounding country" (Luke 7:16–17).

Power over Nature. In the calming of the storm (Luke 8:22–25), Jesus's power over nature is seen. This evokes images of creation and OT acts of power over nature. The exodus included the way through the sea. Power over nature was part of the supernatural deliverance of Israel. Isaiah 51:10, "Was it not you who dried up the sea, the waters of the great deep, who made a road in the depths of the sea so that the redeemed might cross over?" Jesus's power over nature also anticipates the new creation. He was present in the beginning and was the agent of creation (John 1:1), and the

---

13. Green, *Gospel of Luke*, 283.

new creation is also a supernatural event. Jesus was affirming his authority over storm and sea as he did in the exodus.[14]

Forgiveness of Sins

Restoration of Sinners. The feast at Levi's house (Luke 5:27–39) showed immediate fulfillment of the new eschatological era that was in process of being established. So far Jesus has shown mercy to the crippled, the leprous, and now to the social outcast. A banquet in the NT symbolizes joy and points to the eschatological banquet.[15] It is asked why Jesus eats with sinners to which he replies, "I have not come to call the righteous but sinners to repentance." In the question about why he and his disciples do not fast, Jesus refers to his imminent death.

He then proceeded to teach the coming of the new age using a parable. "No one tears a patch from a new garment and sews it on an old one." His mission involves the bringing of a new eschatological era. The second illustration is similar. New wine is not placed in old wineskins for when it ferments it would not be able to be contained. Jesus later speaks of a new covenant. His life and teaching were an invitation to be a part of the remnant that would restore and reunify Israel under the new covenant.

The Good News to the Poor. Green suggests that to understand the Beatitudes in Luke 6:17–49, one must emphasize their ascriptive (and not prescriptive) purpose.[16] By combining wisdom-type Beatitudes with prophetic-type woes they are used to draw the attention of the people to coming disaster stemming from divine judgment. The blessings and (corresponding) woes are present and future. Jesus's new world is eschatological, but it is not relegated to the future. These Beatitudes and woes brought comfort to the ones that Jesus had been already ministering to: lepers, sinners,

14. Liefeld and Pao, "Luke," 161.
15. Liefeld and Pao, "Luke," 124.
16. Green, *Gospel of Luke*, 355.

demonized, toll collectors, women, and so forth. The new world and its values are different from the existing old world. Jesus's ministry (baptism with Spirit) was indicative of what he would do through the church after sending the Spirit (baptism) on the day of Pentecost.

Good News of the Kingdom. The parable of the sower and the lampstand speak of proclaiming the good news of the kingdom. Luke 8:1–15 begins with "Soon afterward, Jesus began going around from one city and village to another, proclaiming and preaching the kingdom of God." In the parable of the sower, Jesus quotes from Isa 6:9, "though seeing, they may not see; though hearing, they may not understand." This is a prophetic indictment on Israel that was a result of the hardening of their heart and not receiving the message of salvation. Paul states in Rom 11:25, "I do not want you to be ignorant of this mystery, brothers, so that you may not be conceited: Israel has experienced a hardening in part until the full number of the gentiles has come in. And so, all Israel will be saved, as it is written."

Green identifies three motifs in chapter 8.[17] Luke 8:1–3 serves as a heading for the section introducing these. (1) The first motif is the salvific agency of Jesus. Jesus's teaching and power are on display as he spreads the word of God. He is identified as "Master" (v. 24) and "Son of the Most High God" (v. 28), and the people recognize his authority and put their faith in him (8:12, 13, 25–48, 50). This is evidenced by falling before him at his feet (e.g., vv. 28, 35, 41, 47). (2) The second motif in this section is the active presence of diabolic agents and influence. Evil spirits/demons, diseases, and the devil himself signify the presence of evil in this passage (vv. 2, 11, 13, 24, 26–39, 40–56). (3) The third motif is the gathering of followers and the consequent importance of authentic response to Jesus. "Throughout chapter eight emphasis is placed on authentic response to Jesus in the face of recognizing and receiving the

---

17. Green, *Gospel of Luke*, 315.

gracious benefaction he brings."[18] Given the reality that the persons healed or freed from demon possession might have expressed different measures of social ostracism, their inclusion into the new community being formed around Jesus is significant. The lives of the women following and serving Jesus anticipate Luke's description of the early Christian community (e.g., Acts 4:32).

Heading for Jerusalem

Jesus's Exodus Predicted

The transfiguration marks the point of Jesus's turning toward Jerusalem (Luke 9:28-36). The transfiguration evokes different points in the Moses-exodus traditions. Park mentions several: the altered appearance of his face, the cloud, the voice, and the response of terror (Luke 9:29, 34-35). All of these recall the experience at Sinai. Even Peter's suggestion to make booths (Luke 9:33) is an allusion to the Festival of Booths, which recalls the wilderness (Lev 23:43).[19] Also, God's announcement of Jesus as the "chosen one" recalls the description of the Isaianic servant as the chosen one (Isa 41:9; 43:10; 44:1). The command to "listen to Him" is an allusion to Deut 18:15 (LXX), which is applied to Jesus by Peter in Acts 3:22. Luke mentions the topic of the conversation of Jesus with Moses and Elijah as being his "exodus" that would occur in Jerusalem—ἔλεγον τὴν ἔξοδον αὐτοῦ ἣν ἔμελλεν πληροῦν ἐν Ἰερουσαλήν.

Luke tells the story of Jesus as the completion of all that has gone before. Israel's story had yet to reach its climax. Redemption would happen in Jerusalem. In Luke 9:51, Jesus sets his face to go to Jerusalem. During the next chapters, it is mentioned regularly that Jesus was "on the way to Jerusalem" (9:53; 10:1; 13:22, 31; 14:25; 17:11; 18:31; 19:1, 11, 28). In these chapters, Luke's presentation of Jesus as a prophet is prevalent and the new exodus typology is clear. The goal toward which the INE motif aims is Jerusalem.

---

18. Green, *Gospel of Luke*, 316.
19. Park, *Pentecost and Sinai*, 191.

The next section is dominated by the sayings of Jesus, which are addressed to his disciples (discipleship), the crowd (admonitions and call to regeneration), and his opponents—the Pharisees and teachers of the law (parables of rejection). Moessner states, "Given Luke's overall perspective of the movement of salvation from Galilee to Jerusalem and then to the 'end of the earth' (Acts 1:8; 10:37, 39), the setting of a journey is not so anomalous after all."[20] Luke's journeying Jesus seems quite natural given his purpose of the fulfillment of Old Testament promise which moves toward the mission of the church.

Outsiders Coming into the Kingdom

The parable of the good Samaritan (Luke 10:25–37) is related to the INE. After telling the parable, Jesus asks the question: "which of these three do you think proved to be a neighbor to the man who fell into the hands of robbers?" The Jew in the ditch discovered that the Samaritan was his neighbor. By implication, he discovered that the other travelers on the road were not his neighbors. This is not a moral story using the Samaritan/Jew feud. The story had more to do with the temple. Who would benefit when YHWH brought in the kingdom? Outsiders were coming into the kingdom, and insiders were being left out. The complete system of temple and sacrifice would be called into question.[21]

There was a way of being Israel that would be truly and radically faithful to Scripture as summed up in the Shema. The lawyer asked the question in Luke 10:25, "What shall I do to inherit eternal life?" The answer is to follow Jesus in finding a new and radicalized version of Torah observance.[22] The parable serves as an announcement and summons worldwide. Jesus was challenging Israel to be the light of the world—the salt of the earth.

---

20. Moessner, *Luke the Historian of Israel's Legacy*, 207.
21. Wright, *Jesus and the Victory of God*, loc. 6467.
22. Wright, *Jesus and the Victory of God*, loc. 6467.

A True Israelite's Prayer

The first petition is for YHWH to sanctify his name (Luke 11:1–13). Fitzmyer states that this probably echoes the prophecy of Ezek 36:22–28.[23] The prophet was told to instruct the house of Israel that YHWH was about to "vindicate the holiness" of his great name, which had been "profaned among the nations." In restoring Israel and giving it a new heart and spirit, YHWH would be removing it from all pagan uncleanness and making it holy. It would be the means of sanctifying his name.

Wright argues that the prayer comes from what Jesus interpreted the coming of the kingdom to mean.[24] The prayer for the kingdom to come had to do with the inauguration of the new covenant. Those who prayed this prayer were, from Jesus's point of view, becoming true Israelites—those whom the covenant God would vindicate. The prayer for deliverance from the time of trial and the evil one also belongs to Jesus's whole kingdom proclamation, the great announcement that Israel had been longing for. The forgiveness of debts was also related to the INE. It was forgiveness of grievances and debts. The new eschatological age brought redemption, new creation, and forgiveness. It was reminiscent of the year of Jubilee (e.g., Acts 4:34; Deut 15:4).

Keener suggests that the first "Father" of the Lord's prayer forms an *inclusio* with the "Father" in 11:13—the climax to the argument of 11:11–13. The relationship with the loving Father is the basis for the Christian prayer in Luke; and the gift of the Holy Spirit is the most essential object of prayer.[25]

Prophecy of Destruction over Jerusalem

In Luke 13:34–35, Jesus laments over Jerusalem. He says, "Behold, your house is left to you desolate; and I say to you, you shall not see Me until the time comes when you say, 'blessed is He who comes

---

23. Fitzmyer, *Gospel According to Luke*, 899.
24. Wright, *Jesus and the Victory of God*, loc. 6201.
25. Keener, "Prayer for the Spirit," 120.

in the name of the Lord!'" This states that a change was coming. Some Pharisees approached Jesus with information to help him escape death. There was the long-standing tradition regarding the destiny of the prophets to undergo persecution and martyrdom in Jerusalem. There is a contrast between the divine necessity (δει) to go to Jerusalem and Herod's will. Jesus's death is at the same time the act of those who oppose him and an event that is purposed by Jesus himself in fulfillment of God's will. Jerusalem is the place where Jesus must die, for it stands for Israel as a whole.

Fitzmyer recognizes that the tradition was that prophets would meet a violent fate, not that they would necessarily do so in Jerusalem (e.g., Jer 26:20–23; 38:4–6).[26] The emphasis on Jerusalem is Lukan following the INE theme.

There is a reference to the judgment coming upon Israel (baptism with fire), ἰδοὺ ἀφίεται ὑμῖν ὁ οἶκος ὑμῶν—"Behold, your house is abandoned." Louw and Nida define ἀφίημι as "cause or permit a person to leave, to leave behind, to divorce, to abandon."[27] Jesus is referring to the transition from the Jerusalem base for the presence of God to a heavenly one. The presence of God would be transferred from Jerusalem to the church, and thus the abandonment of their house.

Jesus is sent on his exodus to the historical and symbolic center of the nation of Israel (Jerusalem) (19:41–44) with the pronouncement of judgment upon the whole people as he looked over the forsaken city. Jesus moved resolutely toward Jerusalem (Isa 50:4–11) embracing the journey of his exodus/death/departure that had been discussed by Moses and Elijah and Jesus on the mount with lightning, cloud, and a voice from heaven. As he approached the city, he saw the city and wept over it and prophesied of its destruction (Luke 19:41).

---

26. Fitzmyer, *Gospel According to Luke*, 1032.
27. Louw and Nida, "ἀφίημι."

Returning from Exile

Wright explains this parable of the prodigal son in the light of the new exodus expectation. Exile and restoration are the main themes of the parable. Babylon had taken the people into captivity. Even though the people returned to the land, most in Jesus's day regarded the exodus as still future. The people had returned in a geographical sense, but the prophecies of restoration had not yet come true. Israel needed to repent and return to YHWH with all her heart. The story of the prodigal (Luke 15:11–32) implies that the hope of the new exodus was being fulfilled. The return from exile was taking place in Jesus's ministry. Israel's exodus was happening within the ministry of Jesus himself and "those who opposed it were enemies of the true people of God."[28]

The parable of the prodigal son replaces normal first-century history interpretation with a new reading.[29] The son that went away in disgrace corresponds to Israel. Exile and restoration were the main themes. This is what the parable was about. The exile was still pending. The prophecy of restoration had not yet come true. This was about to happen. "YHWH would finally become king and would do for Israel, in covenant love, what the prophets had foretold."[30] The return from the exile was taking place in an extremely paradoxical fashion, in Jesus's ministry. Those who oppose the return to the father were defining themselves as outside the true family.

Coronation Ceremony

One of the reasons Jesus was crucified was because of the meaning behind the triumphal entry (Luke 19:28–44). It is known that he was crucified because he came to die; however, the Jewish leaders were aroused to execute him because of certain words and actions of Jesus. In the final week of his ministry, he entered Jerusalem

---

28. Wright, *Jesus and the Victory of God*, loc. 5428.
29. Wright, *Jesus and the Victory of God*, loc. 5548.
30. Wright, *Jesus and the Victory of God*, loc. 2846.

mounted on a donkey amid shouts of "blessed is the king who comes in the name of the Lord" (Luke 19:38). "This deliberately mimicked Solomon, one thousand years earlier, who also rode the royal mule as part of his declaration of kingship (1 Kgs 1:32–40; Zech 9:9)."[31] The crowd's reaction showed their interpretation of it as related to Ps 118.

The entry into Jerusalem and the cleansing of the temple constituted a messianic demonstration, fulfillment event, and a sign of the messianic restoration of Israel.[32] Jesus performed deliberate actions that had symbolic value. "Within his time and culture, his riding on a donkey over the Mount of Olives, across Kidron, and up to the temple mount spoke more powerfully than words could have done of a royal claim" (Zech 9:9ff; e.g., Gen 49:8–12; Isa 63:2; Ps 72:8; Zech 14:4).[33] His action of cleansing the temple was equally royal. "Jesus performed a dramatic action in the temple, and this action was one of the main reasons for his execution."[34]

It was the king who had ultimate authority over the temple. Since Jesus's action portrayed judgment against the most central symbol of Jerusalem, the entire incident has explicit messianic claims. Jesus's actions indicated that Israel's history had reached the point of decisive destruction and rebuilding.[35]

Luke 19:38 quotes Ps 118 (117 LXX) (e.g., Acts 4:11) revealing that the goal of the INE was to reach Jerusalem/Zion (Isa 35:10; 40:9; 51:11), where YHWH's glory would be revealed (Isa 40:5; 52:10), and where he would be made king (Isa 52:7). Hahn emphasizes the priority of Jerusalem for Luke.[36] For Luke, it is theologically important that the word of God go forth from Jerusalem to the ends of the earth (Luke 24:47; Acts 1:8; e.g., Isa 2:3).

---

31. Evans and Wright, *Jesus, the Final Days*, 5.

32. Wright, *Jesus and the Victory of God*, loc. 25804; Hengel and Shwemer, *Jesus and Judaism*, 584; Sanders, *Jesus and Judaism*, 306.

33. Wright, *Jesus and the Victory of God*, loc. 10240.

34. Bockmuehl, *This Jesus*, 60.

35. Wright, *Jesus and the Victory of God*, loc. 10278.

36. Hahn, "Kingdom and Church in Luke-Acts," 303.

Luke inserts ὁ βασιλεὺς[37] in 19:38 in order to relate the citation from Psalms to the prophecy in Zech 9:9.

The Coming Baptism with Fire

The parable of the wicked tenants in Luke 20:9–19 is significant. In the parable, Israel is the vineyard; her rulers are the vineyard-keepers; the prophets are the messengers, and Jesus is the son. This parable has a parallel in Isa 5:1–7. The parable functions as an urgent summons that attempts to break open the worldview of the present tenants and replace it with a new one.[38] In the parable, they kill the son. Afterward, the owner comes and destroys the vine-growers and gives the vineyard to others. They said, "May it never be." He said, "The stone which the builders rejected became the chief cornerstone." The chief priests understood that he was talking about them, and they sought to lay hands on him at that hour, but they feared the people. This is a clear reference to the baptism with fire that was coming upon national Israel.

The New Covenant

The Last Supper (Luke 22:7–38) was the Passover meal that recalled leaving Egypt. To a first-century Jew, it pointed to the return from exile, the awaited new exodus, the covenant renewal spoken of by the prophets.[39] With all of its symbolism—the redemption

---

37. Metzger mentions that others (W 1216 al) omit ὁ βασιλεύς thus bringing the quotation into harmony with its Old Testament original (Ps 118:26) as well as with the synoptic parallels (Matt 21:9; Mark 11:10). The Western text (D it[a,c,d,ff2,i,r1,s]) repeats εὐλογημένος and transposes ὁ βασιλεύς to read quite smoothly εὐλογημένος ὁ ἐρχόμενος ἐν ὀνόματι κυρίου, εὐλογημένος ὁ βασιλεύς. The reading ὁ ἐρχόμενος ὁ βασιλεύς (B arm[(mss)]) being the most difficult accounts best for the origin of the others. Luke emphasizes ὁ βασιλεύς for the triumphal entry. We follow the UBS text for Lukan emphasis on the INE/WOL themes. Metzger and Wikgren, *Textual Commentary on the Greek New Testament*, 170.

38. Wright, *Jesus and the Victory of God*, loc. 3823.

39. Wright, *Jesus and the Victory of God*, loc. 11577.

of the people, victory over Pharaoh, new exodus, forgiveness of sins—this meal was symbolic of Israel's Messiah becoming king. The Last Supper was the meal that brought Jesus's kingdom movement to its climax. It indicated that the new exodus was happening in and through Jesus himself.

Jacob Neusner argues that "the cleansing of the temple and the Last Supper, taken together, indicated that Jesus was in effect intending to replace the temple, as the symbolic focus of Judaism, with his institution meal."[40] The institution meal represented Jesus's death on the cross; therefore, the contrast is between the temple-system and Jesus's ministry.

Wright argues for a comparison between Jesus's actions at the Last Supper and the symbolic actions of Old Testament prophets such as Jeremiah (smashes a pot) or Ezekiel (makes a model of Jerusalem under siege).[41] "As Passover looked back to the exodus and on to the coming of the kingdom, Jesus intended this meal to symbolize the new exodus, the arrival of the kingdom through his fate."[42]

They were celebrating Passover. In the original exodus context, the blood of the lamb was applied to the houses of those who would be redeemed. If the lamb slain in Egypt was the only representative of Jesus—the lamb of God that takes away the sin of the world—then only those who believe in Jesus would be saved from the judgment. The time of the crucifixion was terrible. Darkness fell over the whole land, and the veil of the temple was rent in two. The presence of God would never again be present in the temple of Jerusalem. The holy of holies was no longer a place of God's presence. Judgment had come over national Israel.

---

40. Neusner, "Money-Changers in the Temple," 290.
41. Wright, *Jesus and the Victory of God*, loc. 11616.
42. Wright, *Jesus and the Victory of God*, loc. 11627.

From the Cross to Pentecost

The Crucifixion

In Luke 23:26–56, Luke states that a great number was following him and the women were beating their breasts and wailing for Jesus. He turned to them and said, "Daughters of Jerusalem, stop weeping for me, but weep for yourselves and for your children." Jesus warns them of the fall of Jerusalem. He states, "For if they do these things when the tree is green, what will happen when it is dry?" If Jerusalem deals in this way with the One who came to save Israel—an innocent man during relatively peaceful times—how much more will they do during the coming days of revolution. Josephus records the crucifixion of thousands of Jews during the siege of Jerusalem. The Romans crucified five hundred Jews.[43]

> So the soldiers out of the wrath and hatred they bore the Jews, nailed those they caught, one after one way, and another after another, to the crosses, by way of jest; when their multitude was so great, that room was wanting for the crosses, and crosses wanting for the bodies.[44]

Liefeld and Pao notice that neither Matthew nor Mark mention the incident and attribute purpose in Luke's inclusion of the incident because of his concern for the fate of Jerusalem (e.g., 19:41–44; 21:20–24).[45] The placement of this uniquely Lukan discourse at this point of the narrative serves to emphasize the eschatological nature of the events that are unfolding.

Manek compares the cross to the Red Sea for Israel. Jesus led the new Israel from the earthly Jerusalem to the new Jerusalem and had to go through suffering and the cross. In Luke 12:50 Jesus said, "I have a baptism to undergo, and how distressed I am until it is completed."[46] Isaiah 53 is a clear reference to the cross. It is a clear declaration of redemption through Jesus's ties in the INE with

---

43. Luke 2:22.
44. Josephus, *Works of Flavius Josephus*, 1:405.
45. Liefeld and Pao, "Luke," 334.
46. Manek, "New Exodus in the Books of Luke," 24.

the life and ministry of Jesus. Manek states, "The exodus became a source for understanding history" both historic and prophetic.[47]

The Sending of the Spirit

On the Road to Emmaus

On the road to Emmaus, about seven miles from Jerusalem, two men were talking as they traveled along (Luke 24:13–35). Jesus asked them what they were talking about. Jesus said to them, "'How foolish you are, and how slow of heart to believe all that the prophets have spoken! Did not the Christ have to suffer these things and then enter his glory?' Then beginning with Moses and with all the Prophets he explained to them the things concerning himself in all the Scriptures" (Luke 24:25–27). In Luke 24:44 when gathered with the Twelve, he stated it differently, "These are my words which I spoke to you while I was still with you, that all things which are written about me in the Law of Moses and the Prophets, and the Psalms must be fulfilled." All of the promises of deliverance and restoration of Israel are fulfilled in Christ. It is the new covenant promise of the Spirit that includes the blessings for the nations of the world through the descendants (restored remnant of Israel) of Abraham.

Stay in the City

In Luke 24:44–49, Jesus commanded his disciples to stay in the city. Jerusalem is the key city for the INE. There is a parallel between Luke 24:47 and Acts 1:8. Both contain a mandate to stay in Jerusalem to wait for the coming of the Holy Spirit so that they might receive power and go from there to the ends of the earth. In Acts 1:8, the phrase ἕως ἐσχάτου τῆς γῆς occurs. According to Pao, this phrase is used four times in Isaiah (LXX).[48] The closest in

---

47. Manek, "New Exodus in the Books of Luke," 13.
48. Pao, *Acts and the Isaianic New Exodus*, 89.

context is Isa 49:6. This verse is quoted in Acts 13:47. It seems clear that Luke is quoting Isa 49:6 in Luke 24:27. Through the three infinitives present in Luke 24:46, 47 (παθεῖν, ἀναστῆναι, κηρυχθῆναι), there is a fusion between the ministry of Jesus and that of the apostles.

> And He said to them, "Thus it is written, that the Christ should suffer and rise again from the dead the third day; and that repentance for forgiveness of sins should be proclaimed in His name to all the nations—beginning from Jerusalem." (Luke 24:46, 47)

> He says, "It is too small a thing that you should be my servant, to raise up the tribes of Jacob, and to restore the preserved ones of Israel; I will also make you a light of the nations, so that My salvation may reach to the end of the earth." (Isa 49:6)

But You Shall Receive Power

Acts 1:8 is programmatic for the narrative of Acts. The text of Isa 49:6 is the basis for it, and also Isa 32:15, which suggests the coming of the Spirit signifying the coming new age (e.g., Isa 42:1; 61:1–2). Sweeney claims that Isa 32 played a key role in defining the expectations expressed in Isa 40–55.[49] "Till the Spirit is poured upon us from on high, and the desert becomes a fertile field, and the fertile field seems like a forest." Between the pouring out of the Spirit and the end of the age is the time of the INE.

Pao argues that Acts 1:8 depicts three stages in the program of the INE. "In his selection of traditional material, Luke constructs the development of the early Christian movement within the framework of the Isaianic new exodus to lay claim to the ancient Israelite tradition."[50] The three categories of Acts 1:8 correspond to the INE: (1) the dawn of salvation upon Jerusalem; (2)

---

49. Sweeney, *Isaiah 1–39*, 419–20.
50. Pao, *Acts and the Isaianic New Exodus*, 93.

the reconstitution and reunification of Israel; (3) the inclusion of the gentiles within the people of God.

In Acts 1:8, "power" is mentioned. Luke regularly associates "power" with miraculous healing (Luke 5:17; 6:19; 8:46; 9:1; Acts 6:8; 10:38). The witnesses of Jesus—both the original ones and subsequent ones (Acts 14:3)—would bear witness backed by the Spirit's power, which could frequently include miracles.[51] The Spirit would empower for witnessing to the ends of the earth (Luke 12:11–12; 21:13–15).

Capstone of the INE

The "capstone" of the INE means that Jesus had completed the process of restoration of Israel through redemption on the cross, sending the Spirit to be a blessing to Israel and to the nations of the world. As to the content of the baptism, Luke uses "filled" with the genitive of content to indicate the filling of the Spirit (see table 4). The use of πίμπλημι (fill) to refer to the baptism with the Spirit that occurs on the day of Pentecost is indicative of Luke's emphasis on the Spirit as the capstone of the INE. It signified the presence of God in the new temple (the church both collectively and as individuals) and the commission to continue as the remnant in the mission laid out in Isaiah to the ends of the earth. As to the means, it is discussed above that Luke uses ἐν + dative of means when speaking of the baptism with the Spirit thus supporting Jesus's entire ministry—both as Savior and baptizer—and unifying the process into one multidimensional gospel event.

Table 4. Luke's Use of πλίμπημι + Genitive	
Luke 1:15	πνεύματος ἁγίου πλησθήσεται (gen)
Luke 1:41	ἐπλήσθη πνεύματος ἁγίου (gen)
Acts 2:4	ἐπλήσθησαν πάντες πνεύματος ἁγίου (gen), καὶ ἤρξαντο λαλεῖν ἑτέραις γλώσσαις

---

51. Keener, *Acts: Exegetical Commentary*, 1:691.

Acts 3:10	καὶ ἐπλήσθησαν θάμβους (gen) καὶ ἐκστάσεως (gen) ἐπὶ τῷ συμβεβηκότι αὐτῷ
Acts 4:8	τότε Πέτρος πλησθεὶς πνεύματος ἁγίου (gen)εἶπεν πρὸς αὐτούς
Acts 4:31	καὶ ἐπλήσθησαν ἅπαντες τοῦ ἁγίου πνεύματος (gen)
Acts 5:17	ἐπλήσθησαν ζήλου (gen)
Acts 9:17	ὅπως ἀναβλέψῃς καί πλησθῇς πνεύματος ἁγίου (gen).
Acts 13:9	ὁ καὶ Παῦλος, πλησθεὶς πνεύματος ἁγίου (gen)
Acts 13:45	τοὺς ὄχλους ἐπλήσθησαν ζήλου (gen) καὶ ἀντέλεγον τοῖς ὑπὸ Παῦλος

Luke uses the phrase "filled" with the Spirit (more than any other expression[52]) to describe the baptism experience. Πληρόω occurs eighty-six times in the New Testament. Both Luke and Paul use the word regarding being filled with the Spirit (Acts 13:52; Eph 5:18). Luke uses a cognate term of πληρόω to describe Jesus, the seven deacons, Stephen, and Barnabas as "full of the Holy Spirit." The word πίμπλημι is exclusively Lukan[53] and means to "fulfill" and to "fill." It describes people being filled with the Holy Spirit (Luke 1:15, 41, 67; Acts 2:4; 4:8, 31; 9:17; 13:9).

The Sermons in Acts

Park states that when Luke describes the descent of the Spirit, he uses terms that are meant to recall Sinai.[54] This would be in accord with the fusion of Abrahamic, Mosaic, and Davidic characteristics of the INE. The day of Pentecost with the outpouring of the Spirit has a significance to both the power to preach to the ends of the earth as well as the signs and wonders necessary as each situation arises. To confirm the belief of the early church with regard to the

---

52. In the LXX the term is used over a hundred instances, meaning "to fill," "to satisfy," or, of time, "to run out," "to end." It is used of God's glory filling the house, referring to God's coming or holiness. Delling, "Pleres," 867–72.

53. Except for Matt 23:10; 27:48; Stronstad, *Spirit, Scripture, and Theology*, 81.

54. Park, *Pentecost and Sinai*, 216.

new eschatological age introduced by Jesus, the speeches of Acts are studied as representative of the teaching of the disciples.

The words that Luke attributes to each of the characters in Acts are taken as representing the theology of the early church. If the words of the speeches had been too far out of character with the people they are ascribed to, it would have affected its acceptance by the rest of the church.

I. H. Marshall says,

> We cannot prove that Luke has recorded verbatim what Peter said on this occasion, and in any case, the speech recorded here is too brief to be a full account of what was said. Nevertheless, we have a good example of the kind of thing that was probably said on this occasion, and there can be no doubt that the speech fits admirably into the situation of the day of Pentecost.[55]

The theological importance of the speeches is not disputed. Johnson focuses on the narrative functions of the speeches. He argues that they are not placed randomly but strategically, to provide Luke's readers at key moments with the interpretation of the story that he is narrating.[56] Hans Bayer concurs, "It becomes apparent that Peter's Pentecost and Temple speeches play a significant role in laying the theological foundation for the unfolding narrative of the Book of Acts."[57] Strauss describes Peter's Pentecost speech as an example of the apostolic proclamation and Paul's sermon at Pisidian-Antioch as an example of the Pauline missionary preaching.[58]

Peter's Sermon (Acts 2:14–36)

In explanation of the Pentecost event, Peter cites Joel 2:28, 29 (3:1, 2 LXX) as promise-fulfillment interpretation. Significantly, Joel alludes to the INE. In Joel 2:28 (3:1, 2 LXX) it says,

55. Marshall, *Acts*, 77.
56. Johnson, *Septuagintal Midrash*, 10.
57. Bayer, "Preaching of Peter in Acts," 257.
58. Strauss, *Davidic Messiah in Luke Acts*, 148.

It will come about after this.
That I will pour out My Spirit on all mankind
And your sons and your daughters will prophesy,
Your old men will have dreams,
Your young men will see visions.

When Peter explains what happened on the day of Pentecost, he quotes Joel 2:28 (3:1, 2 LXX) in a *pesher* interpretation. He ties the promise of the Spirit in Joel with the teaching, life, death, resurrection, and enthronement (Davidic covenant) of Jesus. This is the INE, which includes the restoration, reunification of Israel, and salvation to the gentiles. "For the promise is for you and your children, and for all who are far off, as many as the Lord our God shall call to himself." This is the promise of the Father, which is confirmation that the new exodus had begun. It is the culmination of what Jesus came to do and the inauguration of the new eschatological era.

Joel presents a common INE theme with Isa 2:1; 32:15; 40:5; 44:3; 54:13; 57:19 (also Ezek 39:29).

> Until the Spirit is poured out upon us from on high . . . ." (Isa 32:15)

> Then the glory of the Lord will be revealed, and all flesh will see it together. (Isa 40:4)

> For I will pour out water on the thirsty land and streams on the dry ground; I will pour out My Spirit on your offspring, and My blessing on your descendants. (Isa 44:3)

> And all your sons will be taught of the Lord; And the well-being of your sons will be great. (Isa 54:13)

> Creating the praise of the lips. "Peace, peace to him who is far and to him who is near," says the Lord, "and I will heal him." (Isa 57:19)

> And I will not hide My face from them any longer, for I shall have poured out My Spirit on the house of Israel declares the Lord God. (Ezek 39:29)

Marshall states that the first and main theme of the Joel 3:1–4 (LXX) prophecy is that God is going to pour out his Spirit upon all people, i.e., upon all kinds of people.[59] The universal revelation of the glory/salvation of God is an INE theme mentioned in Isa 40:3–5.[60]

Peter's sermon can be divided into three parts: (1) the Pentecost event as the fulfillment of the prophecy in Joel (Acts 2:14–21); (2) the *kerygma* of Jesus's life, death, resurrection, and exaltation as enabling the fulfilling of the Joel prophecy (vv. 22–36); and (3) Peter's call for repentance (vv. 38–41). The main theme of the speech is Christological, explaining the scriptural significance of Jesus's death, resurrection, and exaltation. These main themes are tied into the coming of the Spirit and the restoration of Israel. In Acts 3:19–21,

> Repent therefore and return, that your sins may be wiped away, in order that times of refreshing may come from the presence of the Lord; and that he may send Jesus, the Christ appointed for you, whom heaven must receive until the period of restoration of all things, about which God spoke by the mouth of his holy prophets from ancient time.

Jesus the Prophet like Moses in Stephen's Speech (Acts 7:2–53)

Luke certifies Stephen as a prophet by Luke's literary depiction of him as a man filled with the Holy Spirit who works signs and wonders among the people (Acts 6:5, 8, 10). He finishes his speech by accusing the leadership of resisting the Holy Spirit and killing the prophets (7:51–52). Keener argues that after 70 CE, Stephen's speech became an explanation for the destruction of the temple.[61] Stephen affirmed in Acts 7 that temple worship was not ad-

---

59. Marshall, *Acts*, 78.
60. Pao, *Acts and the Isaianic New Exodus*, 131.
61. Keener, *Acts: Exegetical Commentary*, 2:412.

equate because Jesus had not been accepted. Temple worship was provisional, not eternal, as the events of 70 CE confirmed. Stephen brings an indictment against the leaders of Jerusalem saying,

> "You men who are stiff-necked and uncircumcised in heart and ears are always resisting the Holy Spirit; you are doing just as your fathers did. Which one of the prophets did your fathers not persecute? And they killed those who had previously announced the coming of the righteous one, whose betrayers and murderers you have now become; you who received the law as ordained by angels and did not keep it." Now when they heard this, they were cut to the quick, and they began gnashing their teeth at him.

Judgment upon the wicked priests of Jerusalem had already come at the cross. The presence of God was no longer in the holy of holies of the temple (Luke 23:45), and the Holy Spirit was filling the church to continue with the gathering of the remnant to be a light to the nations.

Paul's Sermon at Pisidian-Antioch (Acts 13:16–41)

As Jesus began his ministry with a sermon in a Jewish synagogue (Luke 4:4–13), Paul also begins his public ministry as a missionary in a synagogue. The first section begins with the phrase "ἄνδρες Ἰσραηλῖται καὶ οἱ ποβούμενοι τὸν θεόν" (v. 16)—"Israelite men and the God-fearers." The second section is also easy to identify because it also begins with a similar phrase, "Ἄνδρες ἀδελφοί, υἱοὶ γένους Ἀβραὰμ καὶ οἱ ἐν ὑμῖν φοβούμενοι τὸν θεόν" (v. 26)—"Men-brethren sons of Abram's lineage and those among us God-fearers." Section three can be identified by a change in person and number. It is the application section. Paul states, "καὶ ἡμεῖς ὑμᾶς εὐαγγελιζόμεθα τὴν πρὸς τους πατέρας ἐπαγγελίαν γενομένην" (v. 32)—"and we ourselves are proclaiming to you the promise which was made to the fathers." Jesus fulfilled the promise made to the fathers.

The first section of the sermon (13:16–25) presents the relation of the mighty acts of God during the exodus from Egypt, the conquest of Canaan, the judges to Samuel, King David ("ἄνδρα κάτα καρδία μου" [v. 22]—"a man according to my heart") to the eschatological deliverance that comes through Jesus. In this sermon, Paul identifies Jesus as the descendant of David—the one who—ὁ θεός ἀπὸ τοῦ σπέρματος κατ᾽ ἐπαγγελίαν ἤγαγεν τῷ Ἰσραήλ σωτῆρα Ἰησοῦν (v. 23)—"From the offspring of this man according to promise, God has brought to Israel a Savior, Jesus." In this section, John the Baptist is quoted as saying, "ἀλλ᾽ ἰδού ἔρχεται μετ᾽ ἐμὲ οὗ οὐκ εἰμὶ ἄξιος τὸ ὑπόδημα τῶν ποδῶν λῦσαι" (v. 25)—"but behold one is coming after me the sandals of whom I am not worthy to untie."

The second section (13:26–31) focuses on the climax of salvation history. Although Israel judging (him) fulfilled (κρίναντες ἐπλήρωσαν, v. 29) the Scriptures of the savior promised by God, "ὑμῖν ὁ λόγος τῆς σωτηρίας ταύτης ἐξαπεστάλη"—"to us the word of this salvation has been sent" (v. 26), after they murdered (ἀναιρεθῆναι) him, they put him in a tomb, but God raised him from the dead. There were witnesses to this.

The third section (13:32–37) lists three OT promises regarding the resurrection of the Son of God (13:33 [Ps 2:7]; 13:34 [Isa 55:3]; 13:35 [Ps 16:10]). In the first, Ps 2:7, Paul identifies Jesus, the descendant of David, as the Son of God coming in fulfilment of what God promised Israel. Second, Isa 55:3 emphasizes the faithfulness of God as he fulfills his promises to David (v. 34 [LXX], καί διαθήσομαι ὑμῖν διαθήκην αἰώνιον τὰ ὅσια Δαυίδ τα πιστά—"and I shall ordain with you a covenant eternal according to the sacred faithful things of David." Third, Paul quotes Ps 16:10 to refer to the resurrection of Jesus as a sign for forgiveness of sins and justification.

The concluding section of the sermon (13:38–41) calls for the people to believe in Jesus and his gospel. He exhorts them with five imperative verbs including the ones quoted in Hab 1:5, ἔστω γνωστὸν—"let it be known"; βλέπετε οὖν μὴ ἐπέλθῃ τὸ εἰρημένον ἐν τοῖς προφήταις—"Guard, then that it does not come what was said by the prophets"; ἴδετε οἱ καταφρονηταί—"behold scoffers"; θαυμάσατε—"marvel"; ἀφανίσθητε—"disappear or perish." The gospel he proclaimed did not leave room for refusal. It was a matter of salvation or judgment. This section ends with a quotation from Hab 1:5, one that warns his audience not to follow their leaders in Jerusalem in rejecting the Son. At first, they received the message and then rejected it. In response to the rejection by the Jews, Paul proclaims, "we now turn to the Gentiles" (13:46).

After this statement, Paul quotes Isa 49:6 in justifying his turn to the gentiles (13:47). This text from Isaiah has been cited in the text (Luke 24:47; Acts 1:8), but most remarkable is its connection with Luke 2:32, where the phrase "a light for revelation to the Gentiles" is applied to Jesus. In this context the phrase "this is what the Lord has commanded us" is referring "light" to Paul and Barnabas, who are bringing the gospel to the gentiles. The continuity between the mission of Jesus and his followers is emphasized by the repeated use of Isa 49:6, a verse that describes God's work in an eschatological era.

Paul supplies a brief historical survey designed to introduce the theme of Jesus as the promised offspring of David raised by God to be a savior for Israel (v. 23). He offers scriptural proof for the life and death of Jesus as the fulfillment of the promise to David (vv. 33–37) and calls the hearers to repentance based on this conclusion (vv. 38–41). The account concludes with a description of gentile reception (13:48) and continued Jewish rejection (13:49–52) of the gospel. As they learned from Jesus's instructions to his disciples (Luke 9:5), Paul and Barnabas "shook the dust from their feet" to signify how the Jews are to react to their rejection of the gospel (13:51). All the while, the disciples continue to be "filled with joy and with the Holy Spirit" (13:52).

The INE as the identity story fits as a paradigm for the themes in this sermon. The Abrahamic, Mosaic, and Davidic covenant themes are intertwined with their fulfillment in the life, death, and resurrection of Jesus. The blessing of Abraham as INE theme follows chronologically the rejection by the synagogue Jews. Isaiah 55:5 says, "Behold, you will call a nation you do not know, and a nation which knows you not, will run to you, Because of the Lord your God, even the Holy One of Israel; for He has glorified you."

Luke Records the Ministry of Paul in Acts 19:1–7

Paul came to Ephesus and found some disciples. He said to them, "After you believed did you receive the Holy Spirit?" The aorist participle makes it clear that believing came before or simultaneous with receiving the Holy Spirit.[62] The question itself signifies that "receiving the Holy Spirit" could be certified by the recipient.

Stanley Horton states that they were disciples already.[63] Perhaps this is not viable hermeneutically. These disciples may or may not have been Christians in a post-Pentecostal sense of the term. What they believed is not stated and must be inferred. Since receiving the Spirit was a common, expected experience to all who "repented and were baptized," perhaps he was gauging whether their experience had been real or not. What can be argued is that in the process "receiving the Spirit" is subsequent to repenting and being baptized (Acts 2:38) This is evident by the use of the aorist with ἐλάβετε πιστεύσαντες ("having believed"—past tense antecedent to the verb ἐλάβετε—"did you receive"). Acts 19:2 says, εἶπεν τε πρὸς αὐτούς, Εἰ πνεῦμα ἅγιον ἐλάβετε πιστεύσαντες—"and he said to them, 'Did you receive the Holy Spirit after you believed?'" The aorist participle is meant to have occurred before the main verb occurred.[64] They were baptized in the name of Jesus and, when Paul placed his hands on them, they began to speak in other tongues as evidence of being baptized with the Holy Spirit. It was understood

---

62. Dunn, *Baptism in the Holy Spirit*, and Fee, "Baptism in the Holy Spirit," do not consider that the disciples of Acts 19 were saved.

63. Horton, *What the Bible Says*, 155.

64. Dunn, *Baptism in the Holy Spirit*, quotes Burton to argue that antecedent action was not intended in Acts 19:2. He fails to refer to the complete explanation in Burton. Burton, *New Testament Moods and Tenses*, 59–60, states that the emphasis of the aorist participle is to denote a simple fact; however, for contemporary action it would be normal to use the present participle. A. T. Robertson, *Grammar*, 860–61, allows for the adverbial (circumstantial) use of the aorist to show contemporary action. Wallace, *Greek Grammar Beyond the Basics*, 614, qualifies the contemporaneous use of the aorist participle to be when the main verb is also aorist. Dana and Mantey, *Manual Grammar*, 229–30, state that the time relations of the participle do not belong to the tense but to the sense of the context.

that it was part of believing in Jesus, although logically subsequent. The question implies the possibility of receiving or not receiving the Holy Spirit when believing and also of an evident sign.

A Hardened Heart and Deaf Ears

Acts 28:25–28 quotes from Isa 6 to cap off the book of Acts. Paul travels to Rome to stand trial, but it seems that it is not he who is on trial but the Jews who reject the gospel message. Salvation to the gentiles does not close the door of salvation for the Jews. "For thus the Lord has commanded us, 'I have placed you as a light for the Gentiles, that you should bring salvation to the end of the earth'" (Acts 13:47)—this includes the nation of Israel. Paul's message in Rome was about the kingdom of God and the lordship of Jesus. The position of this theme at the end of Acts shows its importance in Luke's program. Luke emphasizes the continuity of the followers of Jesus with the ancient Israelite traditions and distinctive identity of the community as the people of God. The Isaianic program is the hermeneutical framework in which isolated events of Luke-Acts are interpreted.

Chapter 4

Results and Conclusion

THE PURPOSE OF THE study was to define Holy Spirit baptism in the light of Scripture. The primary point addressed was the relationship between the baptism with the Spirit and the Isaianic new exodus. For Pentecostals, consistency demanded emphasis on Pentecostal baptism being disconnected to salvation to show that it was not included in the conversion-initiation experience; rather was a subsequent experience. This apologetic stance has been the emphasis for much study and has caused the neglect of Luke's main argument. The Spirit in salvation and the Spirit in Pentecostal baptism has become increasingly distant and almost non-existent as a result. It has made the filling of the Spirit an optional, exclusive experience rather than for "you and your children and for those who are far off." The Spirit is integral to the INE from beginning to end, and Pentecostal filling with the Spirit is the capstone of the new exodus.

Luke shows that the events that have transpired "among us" (Luke 1:1) are the fulfillment of the INE. This is the promised new covenant/salvation plan promised by the Father. "The new exodus was the Jewish way of explaining God's plan of salvation."[1]

When considering the purpose of God in history, the new covenant was at the center of God's plan. Isaiah's concept of the

---

1. Aker, "Paraclete," loc. 7481.

covenant to be fulfilled was the structure of Luke's interpretation of the events beginning with the birth of Jesus and continuing with Pentecost and the spread of the gospel message to the ends of the earth. The final eschatological age had arrived. The Abrahamic, Mosaic, and Davidic covenants merge into the new covenant. God's plan from eternity emerges. The first exodus was a model that was ingrained in Israel's worldview for an understanding of what God would do in the consummation of his plan. The new exodus was spiritual. It included the restoration of Israel and the inclusion (blessing) of the gentiles as promised by the Father to Abraham.

When described in Acts 1:5, 8 this baptism with the Holy Spirit caused the disciples to ask about the "restoration of the kingdom to Israel." There was a definite eschatological new covenant fulfillment connected to the baptism with the Holy Spirit. The same expectation was present in John's baptism. "The people were in a state of expectation wondering if he might be the Christ" (Luke 3:15). The Spirit was sent after Jesus's exaltation as Davidic King seated at the right hand of the Father in accord with the coming kingdom of Israel.

The Israelite people understood that the Messiah would be the bearer of the Spirit (Isa 11:1–2; 42:1; 61:1–3) and that the new covenant would be ratified at the outpouring of the Spirit on all of God's people (Ezek 36:26–27; Joel 2:28–32 [3:1–5a LXX]). The coming of the Holy Spirit after the exaltation of Jesus is interpreted in the light of its context (the INE) as part of the initiation rite into the restored Israel. The coming of the new eschatological age marked the judgment upon Israel (baptism with fire) and the pouring out of the Spirit upon the new temple that is the church (the body of Christ). It involved redemption through faith and acceptance of the lordship of Jesus.

Jesus himself pulls three significant realities together. Jesus embraces in himself the existence of the new people of God, the promised messianic king, and the Lord who in the new exodus creates a new Israel. Through the remnant who became the new people of God and evangelized the gentile world, he will gather to himself a people of all nations. This is the new exodus. The new exodus entails deliverance, new creation, and the filling of the Spirit. It is the Spirit in conjunction with Jesus the Messiah that ushers in the new eschatological age. It is this Spirit that brings divine enablement to bring sinners to Jesus. The filling of the Spirit is essential for missions, and missions is the reason for the new covenant.

In Luke, there is emphasis on Jerusalem. An area where classical Pentecostals has fallen short has been in assuming an apologetic stance and failure to explain the major emphasis in Luke: why Jesus must go to Jerusalem. Luke shows that the enthronement, death, resurrection, and ascension of Jesus and coming of the Spirit—all from Jerusalem—denote the arrival of the INE.

Jerusalem is the place for the restoration of Israel. In the city, he will unite Israel and judge between the remnant and the idolatrous leaders in Israel. Early in his ministry, Jesus brings salvation to all Israel and gives time for the whole nation to hear YHWH and to see and experience his signs and wonders. The nation has time to hear what YHWH is doing and will complete in Jerusalem (INE). Luke shows that YHWH was truly gathering his people. The remnant was the focus and then God used them to win other Jews and gentiles. Luke's emphasis on Jerusalem throughout confirms the INE theme as the explanation of events that had happened among them.

The key to the baptism with the Holy Spirit lies in what God promised Israel, especially in Isaiah. He restores Israel. The baptism reveals two parties: the faithful remnant (confirmed by the Spirit upon them) and the Israelites who reject Jesus (starting with the ruling/priestly class) who were far from YHWH. Jesus visits the small towns of all Israel bringing the Isaianic signs and wonders to gather the remnant. The time of deliverance from exile had arrived. The process of baptizing with Spirit and fire describes the work and lordship of Jesus. The work in Jerusalem will involve both. As Jesus entered Jerusalem he said,

> If you had known in this day, even you, the things which make for peace! But now they have been hidden from

> your eyes. For the days shall come upon you when your enemies will throw up a bank before you, and surround you, and hem you in on every side, and will level you to the ground and your children within you, and they will not leave in you one stone upon another, because you did not recognize the time of your visitation. (Luke 19:42–44)

Then he entered the temple and began to cast out those who were selling while he quoted Isa 56:7 (INE).

The book of Acts continues to describe the WOL, and Jesus continues the same ministry through his disciples. The restoration of Israel and light to the nations through the Spirit are all tied into one indivisible plan. Matthew quotes some of the last words of Jesus in the great commission.

> All power has been given to me in heaven and on earth. Go ye therefore and teach all nations baptizing them in the name of the Father, and of the Son, and of the Holy Spirit, teaching them to observe all that I commanded you; and lo, I am with you always, even to the end of the age. (Matt 28:19, 20)

When one repents and accepts the lordship of Jesus, they should expect to be filled with the Holy Spirit, for it is an integral part of the new eschatological age.

This leads to the problem of this dissertation. What is the relationship between the baptism with the Holy Spirit and the Isaianic new exodus? Historically, Pentecostals have not connected Simeon's prophecy in Luke 2 with Acts 2. The Pentecostal position has been more of a result of apologetics and an attempt to maintain its identity. This has driven a wedge between the cross and Spirit baptism. Spirit baptism is the promise of the Father which is the new covenant and includes the cross. It is usually subsequent to salvation but is connected in Jesus's ministry and should be received immediately after regeneration. It can be described as a new eschatological era that includes the INE for Jesus and the remnant of Israel and the new creation (new temple, new Jerusalem) for a light to the gentiles and the glory of Israel.

The remnant was gathered by Jesus (YHWH the messianic king) to be led out of exile. The exodus is for the remnant who as Jews will evangelize the gentiles. Only the Jews are the focus of Luke and in the first chapters of Acts. Jesus visits the towns and villages of Israel gathering the remnant by performing the Isaianic signs and wonders, i.e., the deliverance from exile had arrived as promised by the prophet Isaiah. Early in ministry, Jesus brings YHWH's salvation to all Israel and gives time for the whole nation to hear and see what God is doing and will complete in Jerusalem. The remnant is the focus at first, and then the Spirit is poured out upon the redeemed on the day of Pentecost to win other Jews to Jesus and the gentiles also. Restored Israel (new temple, new Jerusalem) will comprise Jews and gentiles. Jerusalem is important for Luke for it is at Jerusalem that the remnant is saved and the wicked Jewish leaders are judged. This is what God promised in Isaiah. The new Jerusalem emerges, and the new temple is "filled" with the Holy Spirit for mission and power. The veil is torn from the temple in Jerusalem, and the center of God's presence changes to a new temple in the new eschatological era.

Jesus's work was spread out chronologically. The baptism with the Spirit was last preceded by the enthronement of Jesus. The coming of the Spirit on the day of Pentecost represented the completed work. So, when a person enters the new covenant through the experience, he or she receives the results of what Jesus accomplished in his process—Jesus is on the throne, and it is he who is Lord over all. When a person enters the new covenant, it becomes one event in the life of the future follower of Jesus. There is a difference between presence of the Holy Spirit and manifestations of the Spirit. When one is saved he receives new life (born again) by the Spirit, and it is the same Spirit that flows through the life of the believer in different manifestations: conviction, repentance, regeneration, sanctification, love for the lost, etc. The baptism with the Spirit (filling) implies the same "reality" of what is already there. It does not imply that something different came into being. Christians who are not "filled" with the Spirit evangelize the lost because of the new nature that they have through the work of the

Spirit in salvation; however, when they are filled with the Spirit, it becomes heightened. The Spirit is manifested more fully in the believer who is "baptized in the Spirit." "Missions" is embedded in the new life and experience of salvation, but it becomes much more prominent when the Spirit is manifest more. This is probably the reason Luke preferred the word "filling" when writing about the follower of Jesus in the new covenant. He uses the term "baptism" when referring to the metaphor that describes John the Baptist's ministry and Jesus's ministry in contrast. The "filling" of the Spirit is an important manifestation of the Spirit; however, the believer needs to grow in grace, even after being filled with the Spirit. It is the same Spirit at work.

As a part of the INE, Spirit baptism is an event that includes many aspects. At conversion the Spirit is the means of the new birth and is in the believer, but he manifests himself in different ways. The Pentecostal baptism is part of a process of manifestations of one and the same Spirit. It begins with conviction and repentance and continues with regeneration and making Jesus Lord of one's life. Jesus is the Savior and baptizer, both through the Spirit. Being "filled with the Holy Spirit" is logically "subsequent" to regeneration but is joined to it as part of a multidimensional baptism. The baptism with the Holy Spirit is the promised new covenant/new exodus/new creation.

This dissertation argues the following:

1. The renewal that Isa 40 promises is fulfilled in Luke 2:21 in Simeon's prophecy (in fact, in all the birth narratives in the witnesses of godly people). Acts 2 and following are part of that fulfillment. The filling of the Spirit is the culmination followed by the Jewish mission to the gentiles. Why then is the filling of the Spirit distinct if it is part of the promise?

2. Luke uses the expression "baptism with the Spirit and fire" to describe Jesus's entire ministry and prefers "filling" to describe Pentecostal baptism throughout Acts. This follows Isaiah in describing the new eschatological age. Spirit baptism is the capstone of the INE. Jesus is both Savior and

baptizer—all through the Spirit. The key to the baptism with the Holy Spirit lies in what God promised Israel, especially in Isaiah. He restores Israel (Jesus himself is the remnant of Israel that gathers more unto himself). Two parties emerge—the remnant that will be the new Israel, and the idolatrous, the Israelite power brokers who are far from YHWH and are judged with fire. The exodus is for the remnant who as Jews will evangelize the gentiles (only Jews are the focus of Luke and the first chapters of Acts). Also, Jesus visits the small towns of all Israel bringing Isaianic signs and wonders—the time of deliverance from exile had arrived (according to the INE).

3. After the resurrection of Jesus, he stayed around preparing for the coming of the Spirit. Old Testament texts always include the overwhelming experience with the Spirit with the new exodus and covenant. Harm has been done by modern Pentecostal theology in isolating the work of the Spirit. It has caused the filling of the Spirit to be considered an optional experience.

4. The new exodus was the biblical/Jewish way of describing God's plan of salvation. The promise to Abraham included the mission to the gentiles. The prophets (especially Isaiah) used the symbols of the first exodus to describe what and how he would provide salvation to all people via the remnant as missionaries. The gospel message includes redemption, new creation, and mission all through the restored Jewish people of God (the church).

5. Jerusalem is important in Luke. Jerusalem is key to the restoration of Israel and the coming of the kingdom (Luke 19:28). In Jerusalem, Jesus unites Israel and also judges (according to Isaiah) between the remnant and the idolatrous leader in Israel. The messianic king of Israel arrived bringing the new Jerusalem (the kingdom of God). When he arrived in Jerusalem, he wept over it and prophetically enacted the coming judgment. The restored Israel (Jerusalem) will comprise Jews

and gentiles. In Jerusalem (the city of David) the remnant is saved and the wicked leaders are judged. The new (spiritual) Jerusalem emerges—no more national Israel. The veil of the temple is rent in two. Jerusalem is key, for it is there (the center of the kingdom and temple) where the kingdom is transformed from earthly to heavenly and the earthly center of power is abandoned and destroyed. The new Jerusalem, new Israel, is the church in the New Testament. The remnant of the Old Testament is joined with New Testament believers when Jesus ascends the throne and sends the Spirit. The old age has been consummated and a new beginning has emerged with the resurrection/exaltation/sending of the Spirit of Christ. This is the plan of God from eternity.

6. The clause "He will baptize you with the Holy Spirit and fire" (Luke 3:16b) refers to Jesus's ministry. It is the new covenant made with Israel and taught by the Isaianic new exodus motif. The new exodus complete with regeneration and subsequent filling of the Spirit is the promised redemption, cleansing, and empowerment for mission. It is the "filling" of the new temple (church), which is characteristic of the new eschatological era.

7. It is evident that the filling of the Spirit occurs after repentance and the lordship of Jesus in one's life. Since it is a multidimensional baptizing with the Spirit (i.e., INE) both regeneration and filling could occur instantaneously as they did in Acts 10:44:

> While Peter was still speaking these words, the Holy Spirit fell upon all those who were listening to the message . . . for they were hearing them speaking with tongues and exalting God. Then Peter answered, "Surely no one can refuse the water for these to be baptized who have received the Holy Spirit as we did, can he?"

The best argument in the light of the data presented in this dissertation is that it is a multidimensional INE Spirit baptism that becomes a reality the moment that the presence of the Spirit transforms the believer and includes many manifestations of the same Spirit.

Conclusion

An examination of Luke's argument has shown that in following the INE as the structure and explanation of the things that had occurred among them, the baptism with the Spirit and fire referred to Jesus's entire ministry. The day of Pentecost events were not an extra but rather the main focus of the INE and new covenant. Luke's main argument is not the gift of the Spirit for prophetic enabling but rather the restoration of Israel through the redeemer and the coming of the new eschatological era bringing light to the nations all through the baptism of Spirit and fire.

"Baptize" is a metaphor for Jesus's entire ministry in the salvation enterprise. It refers to the Spirit's full presence and manifestation in Jesus's work of salvation and missions. On this basis, there can be no separation of the Spirit's work in salvation, and empowerment for missions, etc. The new covenant unites the lordship of Jesus and the work of the Spirit. Through the same Spirit a person is saved and also filled with the Spirit (Pentecostal baptism). There is no separation or theological distinctness.

In the multidimensional work of the Spirit there is conviction of sin and a drawing to Christ (this happens before actual regeneration). The Spirit cleanses those who have faith and gives new life. The new life brings naturally a concern for the lordship of Jesus and a godly nature including a concern for the lost. This includes those who have not been filled or "baptized" with the Spirit. When one is filled with the Spirit, it is heightened and the Spirit is manifested more fully in the believer. "Filling" implies the same "reality" of experience already experienced in a fuller sense. It does not imply something different. The "filling" or baptism with the Spirit is part of the many ways the Spirit works in the believer. These include conviction, regeneration, sanctification, filling or anointing for missions or prophetic gifting, and growing in grace and wisdom. It is the same Spirit making full what the new covenant is about.

Acts 2:38 says, "and Peter said to them, 'Repent, and let each of you be baptized in the name of Jesus Christ for the forgiveness of your sins; and you shall receive the gift of the Holy Spirit.'" This text and Luke's use of the INE to explain the covenant show a logical theological subsequence not a chronological one.

Recommendations for Further Study

This study has incited questions for future research. For example, what does "you shall receive power" mean in the light of the promised Spirit baptism? Some today have tried to separate the miracles and exorcisms from the work of the Spirit and classified them as part of the power of God. This is also a result of an apologetic stance and needs to be addressed.

If the filling—"baptism" with the Holy Spirit—is subsequent but part of the finished work of Jesus, what changes should be made in preaching, teaching, or praxis on the subject? How does the restoration and reunification of Israel affect eschatology? In what ways does the baptism with the Holy Spirit and fire describe the events that are still future?

Bibliography

Aker, Benny C. "Charismata: Gifts, Enablements, or Ministries?" *Journal of Pentecostal Theology* 11:1 (2002) 53–69.

———. "The Paraclete: The Spirit of Prophecy in the Johannine Community." In *Reading St. Luke's Text and Theology: Pentecostal Voices. Essays in Honor of Professor Roger Stronstad*, edited by Riku Tuppurainen, 231–42. Kindle. Eugene, OR: Wipf & Stock, 2019.

Aland, Kurt, et al. *The Greek New Testament*. 4th rev. ed. Stuttgart: Deutsche Bibelgesellschaft, 2006.

Allen, David L. *Lukan Authorship of Hebrews*. Kindle. Nashville: B&H, 2010.

Anderson, Bernard W. "Exodus Typology in Second Isaiah." In *Israel's Prophetic Heritage: Essays in Honor of James Muilenburg*, edited by B. Anderson and W. Harrelson, 177–95. New York: Harper and Brothers, 1962.

Arrington, French. "The Indwelling, Baptism, and Infilling with the Holy Spirit: A Differentiation of Terms." *Pneuma: The Journal of the Society for Pentecostal Studies* 3:2 (Fall 1981) 1–10.

Bauer, Walter, William F. Arndt, and F. Wilbur Gingrich. *The Greek Lexicon of the New Testament and Other Christian Literature*. Chicago: University of Chicago Press, 1957.

Bayer, Hans F. "The Preaching of Peter in Acts." In *Witness to the Gospel: The Theology of Acts*, edited by I. Howard Marshall and David Peterson, 257–74. Grand Rapids: Eerdmans, 1998.

Beale, G. K. *Handbook on the New Testament Use of the Old Testament: Exegesis and Interpretation*. Kindle. Grand Rapids: Baker Academic, 2012.

Beale G. K., and D. A. Carson, eds. *Commentary on the New Testament Use of the Old Testament*. Grand Rapids: Baker Academic, 2007.

Beasley-Murray, George R. "Baptism." In *NIDNTTE* 1:460–467.

Berges, Ulrich F. *The Book of Isaiah: Its Composition and Final Form*. Translated by Millard C. Lind. Sheffield: Phoenix, 2012.

Blomberg, Craig L. "The Historical-Critical/Grammatical View." In *Biblical Hermeneutics: Five Views*, edited by Stanley E. Porter and Beth M. Stovell, 27–47. Downers Grove: IVP Academic, 2012.

Bock, Darrel. *Acts*. Baker Exegetical Commentary on the New Testament. Grand Rapids: Baker Academic, 2007.
———. *Luke 1:1—9:50*. Vol. 1. Baker Exegetical Commentary on the New Testament. Grand Rapids: Baker Academic, 1994.
———. *Luke 9:51—24:53*. Vol. 2. Baker Exegetical Commentary on the New Testament. Grand Rapids: Baker Academic, 1994.
———. "Scripture and the Realization of God's Promises." In *Witness to the Gospel: The Theology of Acts*, edited by I. Howard Marshall and David Peterson, 41–62. Grand Rapids: Eerdman, 1998.
———. *A Theology of Luke and Acts*. Kindle. Grand Rapids: Zondervan, 2012.
Bockmuehl, Markus. *This Jesus: Martyr, Lord, Messiah*. New York: T&T Clark International, 2004.
Bosworth, Fred. *Do All Speak in Tongues?* New York: Christian Alliance, 1917.
Bovon, François. *A Commentary on the Gospel of Luke 1:1—9:50*. Minneapolis: Fortress, 2002.
———. *Luke the Theologian: Fifty Years of Research (1950-2005)*. Waco, TX: Baylor University Press, 2006.
Brown, Colin, ed. *New International Dictionary of New Testament Theology*. Grand Rapids: Zondervan, 1971.
Broyles, Craig C., and Craig A. Evans, eds. *Writing and Reading the Scroll of Isaiah: Studies of an Interpretative Tradition*. Vol. 1. New York: Brill, 1997.
Bruce, F. F. *The International Bible Commentary*. Grand Rapids: Zondervan, 1979.
Burton, Ernest de Witt. *New Testament Moods and Tenses in New Testament Greek*. 2nd ed. Edinburgh: T&T Clark, 1998.
Carson, D. A., and Douglas J. Moo. *An Introduction to the New Testament*. Grand Rapids: Zondervan, 2005.
Childs, Brevard S. *Introduction to the Old Testament as Scripture*. Philadelphia: Fortress, 1979.
———. *The Struggle to Understand Isaiah as Christian Scripture*. Grand Rapids: Eerdmans, 2004.
Chilton, B. *The Isaiah Targum: Introduction, Translation, Apparatus, and Notes*. Edinburgh: T&T Clark, 1987.
Clements, Ronald E. "A Light to the Nations: A Central Theme of the Book of Isaiah." In *Forming Prophetic Literature: Essays on Isaiah and the Twelve in Honor of John D. W. Watts*, edited by W. Watts and Paul R. House, 57–69. Sheffield: Sheffield Academic, 1996.
Clifford, R. J. *Fair Spoken and Persuading: An Interpretation of Second Isaiah*. New York: Paulist, 1984.
Conzelmann, Hans. *A Commentary on the Acts of the Apostles*. Hermeneia. Philadelphia: Fortress, 1987.
Dana, H. E., and Julius R. Mantey. *A Manual Grammar of the Greek New Testament*. Toronto: Macmillan, 1955.
Delling, G. "Pleres [full, complete]." *Theological Dictionary of the New Testament, Abridged in One Volume*. Edited by Gerhard Kittel, Gerhard

Friedrich, and Geoffrey William Bromiley, 867–72. Grand Rapids: Eerdmans, 1985.
Dille, Sarah J. *Mixing Metaphors: God as Father and Mother in Deutero-Isaiah.* JSOT Supplement Series 398.2. London: T&T Clark International, 2004.
Dunn, D. G. *The Baptism in the Holy Spirit.* Kindle. London: SCM, 2010.
———. *Christianity in the Making: Jesus Remembered.* Grand Rapids: Eerdmans, 2003.
———. "Feast of Pentecost." In *New International Dictionary of New Testament Theology*, edited by Colin Brown, 783–87. Grand Rapids: Zondervan, 1971.
Estelle, Bryan D. "The Exodus Motif in Isaiah." Westminster Seminary California, 2008. https://www.wscal.edu/resource/the-exodus-motif-in-isaiah/.
Evans, Craig A. "From Gospel to Gospel: The Function of Isaiah in the New Testament." In *Writing and Reading the Scroll of Isaiah: Studies of an Interpretative Tradition*, edited by Craig C. Broyles and Craig A. Evans, 2:651–92. New York: Brill, 1997.
Evans, Craig, and N. T. Wright. *Jesus, the Final Days: What Really Happened.* Louisville: Westminster John Knox, 2009.
Fee, Gordon. "Baptism in the Holy Spirit: The Issue of Separability and Subsequence." *Pneuma: The Journal of the Society for Pentecostal Studies* 7:2 (1985) 87–99.
———. *God's Empowering Presence: The Holy Spirit in the Letters of Paul.* Peabody, MA: Hendrickson, 1994.
———. *Gospel and Spirit: Issues in New Testament Hermeneutics.* Peabody, MA: Hendrickson, 1991.
Finney, Charles. *The Memoirs of Charles G. Finney: An Autobiography.* Waterford: CrossReach, 2021.
Fitzmyer, Joseph A. *The Gospel According to Luke (X–XXIV): Introduction, Translation, and Notes.* New York: Doubleday, 1985.
Flattery, George M. *The Holy Spirit in the New Testament: Luke and Acts.* Springfield, MO: Global University, 2009.
Gentry, Peter J., and Stephen J. Wellum. *Kingdom Through Covenant: A Biblical Theological Understanding of the Covenants.* 2nd ed. Wheaton, IL: Crossway, 1996.
Green, Joel B. "Discourse Analysis and New Testament Interpretation." In *Hearing the New Testament: Strategies for Interpretation*, edited by Joel B. Green, 229–43. Grand Rapids: Eerdmans, 1998.
———. *The Gospel of Luke.* New International Commentary on the New Testament. Grand Rapids: Eerdmans, 1997.
———. "Salvation to the End of the Earth (Acts 13:47): God as Savior in the Acts of the Apostles." In *Witness to the Gospel: The Theology of Acts*, edited by I. Howard Marshall and David Peterson, 83–106. Grand Rapids: Eerdmans, 1998.

Bibliography

Hahn, Scott W. "Kingdom and Church in Luke-Acts: From Davidic Christology to Kingdom Ecclesiology." In *Reading Luke: Interpretation, Reflections, Formation*, edited by Craig Bartholomew, Joel Green, and Anthony Thiselton, 294–326. Scripture and Hermeneutics 6. Grand Rapids: Zondervan, 2005.

Harris, Sarah. "The Davidic Shepherd King in the Lukan Narrative." PhD diss., University of Otago, Dunedin, New Zealand, 2011.

Hengel, Martin, and Ana Maria Schwemer. *Jesus and Judaism*. Waco, TX: Baylor University Press, 2019.

Hildebrandt, Wilf. *An Old Testament Theology of the Spirit of God*. Peabody, MA: Hendrickson, 1995.

Holdcroft, L. Thomas. "Spirit Baptism: Its Nature and Chronology." *Paraclete* 1 (Fall 1967) 27–30.

Horton, Stanley. *What the Bible Says About the Holy Spirit*. Kindle. Springfield, MO: Gospel Publishing House, 2005.

Hurtado, Larry. "Normal, but Not a Norm: 'Initial Evidence' and the New Testament." In *Initial Evidence*, edited by Gary McGee, 189–201. Peabody, MA: Hendrickson, 1991.

Johnson, Luke Timothy. *Septuagintal Midrash in the Speeches of Acts*. Milwaukee: Marquette University Press, 2002.

Josephus, Flavius. *The Works of Flavius Josephus*. Vol. 1. Translated by William Whiston. Grand Rapids: Baker, 1979.

Kaiser, Walter, Jr. *The Promise-Plan of God: A Biblical Theology of Old and New Testaments*. Grand Rapids: Zondervan, 2008.

Keener, Craig. *Acts*. New Cambridge Bible Commentary. Cambridge, UK: Cambridge University Press, 2020.

———. *Acts: An Exegetical Commentary*. Vol. 1. Grand Rapids: Baker Academic, 2012.

———. *Acts: An Exegetical Commentary*. Vol. 2. Grand Rapids: Baker Academic, 2013.

———. *Gift and the Giver: The Holy Spirit for Today*. Grand Rapids: Baker Academic, 2001.

———. *The Gospel of John*. Grand Rapids: Baker Academic, 2003.

———. "Prayer for the Spirit in Luke 11:1–13." In *Reading St. Luke's Text and Theology: Pentecostal Voices. Essays in Honor of Professor Roger Stronstad*, edited by Riku P. Tuppurainen, 114–34. Eugene, OR: Pickwick, 2019.

Kent, Homer A., Jr. "The New Covenant and the Church." *Grace Theological Journal* 6:2 (1985) 289–98.

Kittel, Gerhard, and Gerhard Friedrich, eds. *Theological Dictionary of the New Testament*. Abridged 1 vol. ed. Grand Rapids: Eerdmans, 1985.

Klein, William W., Craig L. Blomberg, and Robert L. Hubbard Jr. *Introduction to Biblical Interpretation*. Nashville: Thomas Nelson, 2004.

Kovacs, Frank Z. "The Covenant in Luke-Acts." MT diss., North-West University, Potchefstroom, South Africa, 2006.

Bibliography

Kwon, Hyuk J. "Psalm 118 (117 LXX) in Luke-Acts: Application of a 'New Exodus Motif.'" *Verbum et Ecclesia* 30:2 (2009) a59. DOI: 10.4102/ve.v30i2.59.

Leedy, Paul D., and Jeannie Ellis Ormrod. *Practical Research: Planning and Design*. New York: Pearson, 2013.

Leiter, David A. "Visions of Peace in Isaiah." In *Inspired Speech: Prophecy in the Ancient Near East. Essays in Honor of Herbert B. Huffman*, edited by John Kaliner and Louis Stulman, 244–52. JSOT Supplement Series 378. London: T&T Clark International, 2004.

Lessing, R. Reed. "Isaiah's Servant in Chapters 40–55: Clearing up the Confusion." *Concordia Journal* (Spring 2011) 130–34.

Liefeld, Walter. *Interpreting the Book of Acts*. Guides to New Testament Exegesis 4. Grand Rapids: Baker, 1995.

Liefeld, Walter L., and David W. Pao. "Luke." In *The Expositors Bible Commentary* 10, edited by Tremper Longman III and David E. Garland. Rev. ed. Logos online edition. Grand Rapids: Zondervan, 2007.

Lim, Bo H. *The "Way of the Lord" in the Book of Isaiah*. New York: T&T Clark, 2010.

Lohse, Eduard. "Σιών." In *TDNT* 7:320–338.

Longenecker, Richard. "Acts." In *The Expositors Bible Commentary* 10, edited by Tremper Longman III and David E. Garland. Rev. ed. Logos online edition. Grand Rapids: Zondervan, 2007.

Louw, Johannes P., and Eugene A. Nida. *Lexicon of the New Testament Based on Semantic Domains*. 2nd ed. New York: United Bible Societies, 1989.

Manek, Jindrik. "The New Exodus in the Books of Luke." *Novum Testamentum* 2, Fasc. 1 (Jan. 1957) 8–24.

Marshall, I. Howard. *Acts: An Introduction and Commentary*. Tyndale New Testament Commentaries 5. Leicester, England: InterVarsity, 1980.

———. *The Gospel of Luke: A Commentary on the Greek Text*. The New International Greek Testament Commentary. Grand Rapids: Paternoster, 1978.

———. *New Testament Theology: Many Witnesses, One Gospel*. Downers Grove, IL: InterVarsity, 2004.

———. "The Significance of Pentecost." *The Asbury Seminarian* 32:2 (1977) 17–39.

Martin, Larry. *In the Beginning: Readings on the Origins of the Twentieth Century Pentecostal Revival and the Birth of the Pentecostal Church of God*. Duncan, OK: Christian Life Books, 1994.

McGinnis, Claire Mathews, and Patricia K. Tull, eds. *"As Those Who Are Taught": The Interpretation of Isaiah from the LXX to the SBL*. Atlanta: Society of Biblical Literature, 2006.

McKnight, Scot. *The Jesus Gospel: The Original Good News Revisited*. Kindle. Grand Rapids: Zondervan, 2011.

Melugin, Roy F. *The Formation of Isaiah 40–55*. Berlin: de Gruyter, 1976.

Bibliography

Melugin, Roy F., and Marvin A. Sweeney, eds. *New Visions of Isaiah*. Sheffield: JSOT Press, 1996.

Menzies, Robert P. "Luke's Understanding of Baptism in the Holy Spirit." *PentecoStudies* 6:1 (2007) 108–26.

———. "Luke's Understanding of Baptism in the Holy Spirit: A Pentecostal Dialogue with the Reformed Tradition." *Journal of Pentecostal Theology* 16:2 (2008) 86–101.

Menzies, William W., and Robert P. Menzies. *Spirit and Power: Foundations of Pentecostal Experience*. Grand Rapids: Zondervan, 2000.

Metzger, Bruce M., and Allen Wikgren. *A Textual Commentary on the Greek New Testament*. London: United Bible Societies, 1971.

Meyer, Ben F. "The Temple: Symbol Central to Biblical Theology." *Gregorianum* 74:2 (1993) 223–40.

Miller, David. "Luke's Conception of Prophets Considered in the Context of Second Temple Literature." PhD diss., McMaster University, Hamilton, Ontario, 2004.

Moessner, David Paul. *Luke the Historian of Israel's Legacy, Theologian of Israel's Christ: A New Reading of the "Gospel Acts" of Luke*. Berlin: de Gruyter, 2016.

Morphew, Derek. *The Mission of the Kingdom: The Theology of Luke-Acts*. Kindle. Bergvliet, South Africa: Self-published, 2011.

Moyise, Steve, and Menken J. J. Maarten, eds. *Isaiah in the New Testament*. New York: T&T Clark, 2005.

Nelson, P. C. *The Baptism in the Holy Spirit, the Doctrine, the Experience, the Evidence*. Fort Worth, TX: Southwestern, 1942.

Neudorfer, Heinz-Werner. "The Speech of Stephen." In *Witness to the Gospel: The Theology of Acts*, edited by I. Howard Marshall and David Peterson, 275–94. Grand Rapids: Eerdmans, 1998.

Neusner, Jacob. "Money-Changers in the Temple: The Mishnah's Explanation." *New Testament Studies* 35:2 (Apr. 1989) 287–90.

Nolland, John. "Salvation-History and Eschatology." In *Witness to the Gospel: The Theology of Acts*, edited by I. Howard Marshall and David Peterson, 63–82. Grand Rapids: Eerdmans, 1998.

O'Connell, Robert H. *Concentricity and Continuity: The Literary Structure of Isaiah*. JSOT Supplement Series 188. Sheffield: Sheffield Academic, 1994.

Oepke, Albrecht. "βαπτίζω." In *TDNT* 1:530–46.

Oss, Douglas. "A Pentecostal/Charismatic View." In *Are Miraculous Gifts for Today: Four Views*, edited by Stanley N. Gundry and Wayne A. Grudem, 248–305. Grand Rapids: Zondervan, 1996.

O'Toole, Robert F. "Acts 2:30 and the Davidic Covenant of Pentecost." *Journal of Biblical Literature* 102:2 (1983) 245–58.

Palma, Anthony. *The Holy Spirit: A Pentecostal Perspective*. Kindle. Springfield, MO: Logion Gospel Publishing House, 1984.

Park, Sejin. *Pentecost and Sinai: The Festival of Weeks as a Celebration of the Sinai Event*. New York: T&T Clark, 2008.

Bibliography

Pao, David, W. *Acts and the Isaianic New Exodus.* Eugene, OR: Wipf & Stock, 2000.

———. *Commentary on Acts.* The Baker Illustrated Bible Commentary. Kindle. Grand Rapids: Baker, 2012.

Pervo, Richard I. *Acts: A Commentary.* Hermeneia. Minneapolis: Fortress, 2009.

Polhill, John B. *Acts.* The New American Commentary. Nashville: Broadman and Holman, 1992.

Porter, Stanley. *The Messiah in the Old and New Testaments.* Grand Rapids: Eerdmans, 2007.

Porter, Stanley E., and Beth M. Stovell, eds. *Biblical Hermeneutics: Five Views.* Downers Grove, IL: IVP Academic, 2012.

Reist, Irwin W. "The Theological Significance of the Exodus." *Journal of the Evangelical Theological Society* 12:4 (1969) 223–32.

Ridout, Samuel. *The Collected Works of Samuel Ridout.* N.p.: Jawbone Digital, 2013.

Riggs, Ralph M. *The Spirit Himself.* Kindle. Springfield, MO: Gospel Publishing House. 1977.

Roberts, J. J. M. "Isaiah in Old Testament Theology." In *Interpreting the Prophets,* edited by James Luther Mays and Paul J. Achtemeier, loc. 995–1151. Kindle. Philadelphia: Fortress, 1987.

Robertson, A. T. *A Grammar of the Greek New Testament in the Light of Historical Research.* Nashville: Broadman, 1934.

Robinson, H. Wheeler. *Corporate Personality in Ancient Israel.* Philadelphia: Fortress, 1964.

Ross, Stuart. "Luke-Acts and the Gentile Mission." Unpublished paper presented to Regent University School of Divinity, 2016.

Ruthven, Jon. "'This Is My Covenant with Them': Isaiah 59.19–21 as the Programmatic Prophecy of the New Covenant in the Acts of the Apostles (Part I)." *Journal of Pentecostal Theology* 17 (2008) 32–47.

———. "'This Is My Covenant with Them': Isaiah 59.19–21 as the Programmatic Prophecy of the New Covenant in the Acts of the Apostles (Part II)." *Journal of Pentecostal Theology* 17 (2008) 219–37.

Ryken, Leland. *Words of Delight: A Literary Introduction to the Bible.* Grand Rapids: Baker Academic, 1992.

Sanders, E. P. *Jesus and Judaism.* Philadelphia: Fortress, 1985.

Sanders, James. "Isaiah in Luke." In *Interpreting the Prophets,* edited by James Luther Mays and Paul J. Achtemeier, loc. 1156–321. Kindle. Philadelphia: Fortress, 1987.

Schweizer, Eduard. "πνεῦμα." In *TDNT* 6:407–8.

Seccombe, David. "Luke and Isaiah." *New Testament Studies* 27:2 (1981) 252–59.

Shalom, Paul. *Isaiah 40–66 Translation and Commentary.* Grand Rapids: Eerdmans, 2012.

Shelton, James B. *Mighty in Word and Deed.* Eugene, OR: Wipf & Stock, 2000.

Silva, Moisés. "Ἰερουσαλήμ. Jerusalem." In *NIDNTTE* 2:522–27.

———, ed. *New International Dictionary of New Testament Theology and Exegesis*. Vols. 1–5. Grand Rapids: Zondervan, 2014.

———. "πεντηκοστή. Pentecost." In *NIDNTTE* 3:708–13.

Spencer, F. Scott. "The Literary Postmodern View." In *Biblical Hermeneutics: Five Views*, edited by Stanley E. Porter and Beth M. Stovell, 48–69. Downers Grove, IL: IVP Academic, 2012.

Stargel, Linda. *The Construction of Exodus Identity in Ancient Israel*. Kindle. Eugene, OR: Pickwick, 2018.

Stott, John. *Baptism and Fullness: The Work of the Holy Spirit Today*. 3rd ed. Kindle. Downers Grove, IL: InterVarsity, 2006.

Strauss, Mark. *The Davidic Messiah in Luke Acts*. JSNT Supplement Series. Sheffield: Sheffield Academic, 1995.

———. *Luke*. Zondervan Illustrated Bible Backgrounds Commentary. Kindle. Grand Rapids: Zondervan, 2002.

Strauss, Stephen J. "The Purpose of Acts and the Mission of God." *Bibliotheca Sacra* 169 (Oct.–Dec. 2014) 443–64.

Strong, Augustus H. *Systematic Theology*. Valley Forge, PA: Judson, 1993.

Strong, James. *The New Strong's Concise Dictionary of the Words in the Greek Testament and the Hebrew Bible*. Bellingham, WA: Logos Bible Software, 2009.

Stronstad, Roger. *The Charismatic Theology of St. Luke*. Peabody, MA: Hendrickson, 1984.

———. *The Prophethood of All Believers: A Study in Luke's Charismatic Theology*. Springfield, MO: Global University, 1998.

———. *Spirit, Scripture, and Theology: A Pentecostal Perspective*. Baguio City, Philippines: Asia Pacific Theological Seminary Press, 1995.

Squires, John. "The Plan of God in the Acts of the Apostles." In *Witness to the Gospel: The Theology of Acts*, edited by I. Howard Marshall and David Peterson, 17–36. Grand Rapids: Eerdmans, 1998.

Swanson, James. *A Dictionary of Biblical Languages with Semantic Domains: Greek New Testament*. Oak Harbor, WA: Logos Research Systems, 1977.

Sweeney, Marvin A. *Isaiah 1–39 with Introduction to Prophetic Literature*. The Forms of the Old Testament Literature 26. Grand Rapids: Zondervan, 1996.

Tannehill, Robert C. *The Narrative Unity of Luke-Acts: A Literary Interpretation*. Vol. 1: *The Gospel According to Luke*. Kindle. Philadelphia: Fortress, 1986.

Turner, Max. *Power from on High: The Spirit in Israel's Restoration and Witness in Luke-Acts*. Journal of Pentecostal Theology: Supplement Series 9. Sheffield: Sheffield Academic, 1996.

———. "The Spirit and the Power of Jesus's Miracles in the Lucan Conception." *Novum Testamentum* 33, Fasc. 2 (Apr. 1991) 124–52.

———. "The Spirit in Luke-Acts: A Support or a Challenge to Classical Pentecostal Paradigms?" Presentation to the Pentecostal and Charismatic Research Fellowship, Dec. 1996.

———. "The Spirit of Prophecy and the Power of Authoritative Preaching in Luke-Acts: A Question of Origins." *New Testament Studies* 38 (1992) 66–88.

———. "The 'Spirit of Prophecy' as the Power of Israel's Restoration and Witness." In *Witness to the Gospel: The Theology of Acts*, edited by I. Howard Marshall and David Peterson, 327–48. Grand Rapids: Eerdmans, 1998.

———. "The Work of the Spirit in Luke-Acts." *Word and World* 23:2 (2003) 146–53.

Unger, Merrill. *The Baptism and Gifts of the Holy Spirit*. Chicago: Moody, 1974.

VanderKam, James C. "Covenant and Pentecost." *Calvin Theological Journal* 37:2 (2002) 239–54.

Vlach, Michael J. "Various Forms of Replacement Theology." *The Master's Seminary Journal* 20:1 (Spring 2009) 57–69.

Wallace, Daniel. *Greek Grammar Beyond the Basics*. Grand Rapids: Zondervan, 1996.

Wardle, Timothy. *The Jerusalem Temple and Early Christian Identity*. Tubingen: Mohr Siebeck, 2010.

Watts, James W., and Paul R. House, eds. *Forming Prophetic Literature: Essays on Isaiah and the Twelve in Honor of John D. W. Watts*. The Library of Hebrew Bible Old Testament Studies. Sheffield: Sheffield Academic, 1996.

Watts, Rikk. *Echoes from the Past: Israel's Ancient Traditions and the Destiny of the Nations in Isaiah 40–55*. Vancouver: Regent College, 2004.

———. *Isaiah's New Exodus in Mark*. Grand Rapids: Baker Academic, 1997.

Webb, Robert. "Jesus' Baptism by John: Its Historicity and Significance." In *Key Events in the Life of the Historical Jesus: A Collaborative Exploration of Context and Coherence*, edited by Darrell L. Bock and Robert L. Webb, 95–150. Tubingen: Mohr Siebeck, 2009.

Westermann, Claus. *Isaiah 40–66*. Translated by David M. G. Stalker. Göttingen: Vandenhoech & Ruprecht, 1969.

Wilms, Glen H. "Deuteronomic Traditions in Luke's Gospel." PhD diss., University of Edinburgh, 1972.

Witherington, Ben, III. *Acts: A Socio-Rhetorical Commentary*. Grand Rapids: Eerdmans, 1978.

Wright, N. T. *Jesus and the Victory of God*. Kindle. Great Britain: Society for Promoting Christian Knowledge, 1996.

———. *The New Testament and the People of God: Christian Origins and the Question of God*. Vol. 1. Great Britain: Society for Promoting Christian Knowledge, 1992.

Wyckoff, John W. "The Baptism in the Holy Spirit." In *Systematic Theology*, edited by Stanley Horton, loc. 9420–10162. Kindle. Springfield, MO: Gospel Publishing House, 2007.

www.ingramcontent.com/pod-product-compliance
Lightning Source LLC
Chambersburg PA
CBHW072144160426
43197CB00012B/2241